Written Standard Chinese

Volume One

Parker Po-fei Huang and
Hugh M. Stimson

Far Eastern Publications
Yale University

TABLE OF CONTENTS

Introduction

Introduction

Written Standard Chinese, in two volumes (WSC I and WSC II), introduces six hundred common characters in thirty lessons, twenty characters per lesson, fifteen lessons per volume. It is designed to be used with Spoken Standard Chinese, also in two volumes (SSC I and SSC II), by the present authors (New Haven: Far Eastern Publications, 1976 and 1978, respectively). In each lesson, the characters are first introduced in their "complicated" forms (fántǐzǐ), which were the official forms in China before 1949, and which are still official on Taiwan. Important variant forms, and the "simplified forms" (jiǎntǐzǐ) which have been official in mainland China since 1949, are also given in each lesson.

WSC I is designed to be used with SSC I and the first two lessons of SSC II. We intend the student to begin Lesson 1 of WSC I after he has finished Lesson 2 of SSC I; Lesson 1 of WSC I uses only vocabulary and grammar that appear in the first two lessons of SSC I. Similarly, Lesson 2 of WSC I presupposes Lesson 4 of SSC I, Lesson 3 of WSC I presupposes Lesson 5 of SSC I, and so on. After the title of each lesson in WSC I we give the lesson in SSC I or II which the WSC I lesson presupposes.

Each lesson begins with a preparatory section. The first part of this section includes a brief review of any grammar covered in the presupposed lessons of SSC I or II which appears in the WSC I lesson for the first time. Those studying SSC I and II at the same time as WSC I will find this part of the preparatory section useful as a review; students using WSC I alone will find this part essential for an understanding of the material in the WSC I lesson.

Next in the preparatory section is a chart displaying the twenty new characters of the lesson in their unsimplified form. Numbers beside the strokes of each character show the order and direction of the strokes. Beneath each character are a number

giving the total number of strokes in the character, a radical-
remainder code, and the radical in the shape that it takes when
it appears alone. Variant and simplified forms are similarly
presented next in this section. Finally, common radicals appearing for the first time in the new characters are pointed
out and briefly explained.

In the following section, the characters are introduced
as vocabulary items, including pronunciation (in pīnyīn roman-
ization), indications of grammatical function, English glosses,
and, where appropriate, words and phrases in which they appear.
Following this main vocabulary is another vocabulary introducing
new uses for characters that have already been introduced in
earlier lessons. Occasionally new words and usages appear in
WSC I which do not appear in the presupposed SSC lessons; these
are marked with asterisks.

The rest of the lesson is devoted to presenting the new
characters, first in very short contexts, such as phrases and
short sentences, then in longer contexts, such as longer sentences,
dialogs, and stories. The last part of the lesson presents part
of the preceding material in simplified characters.

Parker Po-fei Huang
Hugh M. Stimson

Written Standard
Chinese

WRITTEN STANDARD CHINESE

Volume One

Lesson 1

I.   Preparation

1.1 <u>Grammar review.</u> The following is a summary of the grammatical
points introduced in Lessons 1 and 2 of <u>Spoken Standard Chinese</u> (SSC 1-2).

Chinese grammar can be described in terms of parts of speech, grammatical
relationships, and patterns. Parts of speech are groups of morphemes--words
and meaningful elements smaller than words--which share common privileges of
occurrence. As they occur in sentences, morphemes and groups of morphemes
function as constituent parts of the sentences in which they occur. There are
five grammatical relationships that obtain between parts of a sentence in
Chinese: topic-comment, modifier-modified, co-ordinate, verb-object, and appositive. Parts of speech and grammatical relationships combine to make up
the many sentence and phrase patterns used in speaking and writing the Chinese
language.

1.1.1 <u>Parts of speech.</u> Chinese morphemes are classified first of all
according to whether or not they ever occur alone as sentences. A morpheme
that occurs as a sentence is a <u>free form</u>, whereas one that only occurs attached
to other morphemes is a <u>bound form</u>. The bound forms introduced in SSC 1-2 are
fixed adverbs, particles, and otherwise unclassified boundforms. The free
forms introduced in these lessons are nouns, stative verbs, and functive verbs.

1.1.1.1 <u>"A" fixed adverbs</u> (S 1.N5, 1.6, 4.10).* An adverb is a bound
form attached to a following comment. A fixed adverb is an adverb that always
immediately precedes a verb or another fixed adverb. In the following examples,
<u>hǎo</u> "good" is a stative verb, and <u>bù-</u> "not", <u>hěn</u> "very", and <u>zhēn</u> "really" are
fixed adverbs. The Chinese examples are acceptable as complete sentences,

---

*Material in SSC is located by a code which gives, after "S", first the
lesson number, the the section or footnote containing the material. "N"
stands for "note to the 'New Words' section".

1

unspecified as to tense, and with no indication of the subject of the stative
verb.   Thus many translations into English are possible, of which the ones
with "it's" are perhaps closest to the vagueness of the Chinese.   In general
English versions of the Chinese examples in this text are representative
rather than definitive.

好。	hǎo.	It's good.
不好。	bùhǎo.	It's not good.
很好。	hěn hǎo.	It's very good.
真好。	zhēn hǎo.	It's really good.
不很好。	bùhěn hǎo.	It's not very good.
真不很好。	zhēn bùhěn hǎo.	It's really not very good.

1.1.1.2 "P" particles (S 1.N7, 1.8) are bound to phrases or sentences
that precede them.   ma is an interrogative particle.

| 好嗎? | hǎo ma? | Is it good? |
| 不好嗎? | bùhǎo ma? | Isn't it good? |

1.1.1.3 "BF" otherwise unclassified bound forms (S 2.N5). The noun
suffix -men is a bound form that adds plural meaning to the preceding Chinese
words, which correspond to the English personal pronouns.

我	wǒ	I, me
我們	wǒmen	we, us
你	nǐ	you (singular)
你們	nǐmen	you (plural)

1.1.1.4 "N" nouns (S 1.N3). A definition of the term "noun" in terms of
privileges of occurrence will appear in the next chapter, after certain other
parts of speech are introduced. Chinese nouns are like English ones, except
that Chinese nouns are intrinsically ambiguous as to number and specificity.

| 書 | shū | a book, the book, books, the books |
| 報 | bào | a newspaper, the newspaper, newspapers, the newspapers |

Substituting for nouns, and classed as nouns in these materials, are words corresponding to the English personal pronouns. These words are marked as to number: they are singular if not suffixed with -men, and they are plural if they are so suffixed.

1.1.1.5 "SV" stative verbs (S 1.N4). A verb in Chinese is a free form that sometimes occurs with a negative prefix, like bù-, and is intrinsically ambiguous as to tense, person, and number. A stative verb, in addition to occurring with bù-, also occurs with certain intensifying bound forms, such as hěn "very". For examples see 1.1.1 above.

A lone stative verb, not preceded by an intensifying adverb, is not only ambiguous as to tense, person, and number, but is also ambiguous as to whether or not comparison is intended. Thus the sentence hǎo, means either "It is good." or "It is better." The addition of an intensive adverb blocks the comparison alternative. Thus the sentence hěn hǎo. means only "It is good."

1.1.1.6 "V" functive verbs (S 2.N8) are verbs that do not occur with certain intensive bound forms (specifically the intensive suffixes) and which occur with verbal suffixes (see later chapters).

| 買 。 | mǎi. | She's buying it. |
| 不買 。 | bùmǎi. | She's not buying it. |

1.1.2 Grammatical relationships. The grammatical relationships introduced in SSC 1-2 are topic-comment, modifier-modified, co-ordinate, and verb-object.

1.1.2.1 The topic-comment relationship (S 1.5). In these materials, a Chinese sentence consists of a lone comment, or of a comment preceded by a topic.

The topic expresses old or shared information, and when it is a noun the

English translation often adds the definite article "the". The comment contains new information and is normally the focus of the sentence.

In the examples below, <u>shū</u> "book" is the topic and hence is likely to be specific, so the English versions include "the". The stative verb <u>guì</u> "expensive" is the main word of the comment.

書很貴嗎？	shū, hěn guì ma?	Are the books very expensive?
書很貴。	shū, hěn guì.	The books are very expensive.
很貴。	hěn guì.	They're very expensive.
書不很貴。	shū, bùhěn guì.	The books aren't very expensive.
不很貴。	bùhěn guì.	They're not very expensive.

In a dialog, a positive answer to a question will usually consist of a repetition of the comment in the question, minus the question element (<u>ma</u> in the first example above), with or without the topic. Thus, to <u>shū, hěn guì ma?</u> positive answers may be <u>shū, hěn guì</u> or just <u>hěn guì</u> and are equivalent to the English "Yes." A negative answer will add the negative adverb. Thus, as answers to the same question, <u>shū, bùhěn guì</u> or just <u>bùhěn guì</u> are equivalent to "No."

1.1.2.2 <u>The modifier-modified relationship.</u> Particles and certain suffixal bound forms modify the morphemes or phrases that precede them (S 1.9). The suffix <u>-men</u> modifies <u>wǒ</u> in <u>wǒmen</u> "we, us". The particle <u>ma</u> modifies the preceding phrase in <u>hěn hǎo ma?</u> "Is it very good?"

Otherwise, modifiers precede the morphemes that they modify. Adverbs precede the verbs (or comments) that they modify (S 1.6). In strings of two or more fixed adverbs, the adverb right before the verb modifies the verb, the next adverb modifies the adverb-verb combination that follows it, and so on. Thus, in <u>zhēn bùhěn hǎo</u> "It's really not very good.", <u>hěn</u> modifies <u>hǎo</u>, <u>bù-</u> modifies <u>hěn hǎo</u>, and <u>zhēn</u> modifies <u>bùhěn hǎo</u>. The order of the English words corresponding to the Chinese fixed adverbs may vary. For example, the translation of <u>zhēn</u> "really, indeed" may follow the **translation of the stative**

verb: <u>zhēn hěn hǎo.</u> "It's very good indeed." Such variation in the order
is impossible in Chinese.

Adjacent nouns are sometimes in the modifier-modified relationship; if
so, the first noun modifies the second (S 2.4). In the following examples,
the noun <u>shū</u> "book" is preceded by a noun denoting a country: <u>Zhōngguo</u>
"China" or <u>Měiguo</u> "America". If these modifying nouns are translated as
English adjectives, they precede the modified noun, as in Chinese. But if
they are translated as English phrases or clauses, these are required by the
rules of English grammar to follow the modified noun; this order is impossible
in Chinese.

中國書	Zhōngguo shū	Chinese books / books from China / books written in Chinese
美國書	Měiguo shū	American books / books from America

1.1.2.3 <u>The co-ordinate relationship</u> (S 1.11). Two or more elements in
a co-ordinate relationship are often connected in English by a conjunction
such as "and" or "or". Such overt representation of this relationship is less
frequent in Chinese

The co-ordinate "or" relationship is introduced in SSC 1-2 in connection
with the choice-type question patterns. For example, <u>'Zhongguo shū guì,</u>
<u>'Měiguo shū guì</u>? "Are Chinese books more expensive, or are American books more
expensive?", the two parts separated by a comma are in a co-ordinate "or"
relationship, with "or" not overtly expressed in the Chinese. The English
translation can be compressed: "Which are more expensive, Chinese books or
American ones?"; such compression is impossible in Chinese. See below,
1.1.3.3, for more on the choice-type question.

1.1.2.4 <u>The verb-object relationship</u> (S 2.5). Some functive verbs are
followed by a noun denoting the person or thing affected by the action of the
verb. Such a noun functions as the object "O" of the verb. In the examples

below, <u>shū</u> "book" and <u>bào</u> "newspaper" are nouns functioning as objects of the
preceding functive verbs, <u>mǎi</u> "buy" and <u>kàn</u> "read".

你買書嗎？	nǐ mǎi shū ma?	Are you buying books?
我不買書。	wǒ bùmǎi shū.	I'm not buying books. / No, I'm not.
你看報嗎？	nǐ kàn bào ma?	Do you read newspapers?
我看報。	wǒ kàn bào.	I read newspapers. / Yes, I do.

1.1.3 Patterns.

1.1.3.1 <u>The simple descriptive sentence</u> (S 1.7). The main word of a
simple descriptive sentence is a stative verb. This word is the main word of
the comment, which is optionally preceded by a topic. Within the comment,
the stative verb is optionally preceded by one or more adverbs (1.1.1.1) and
optionally followed by a sentence particle, such as <u>ma</u> (S 1.9, 1.1.1.2).
Using parentheses to enclose symbols for optional elements and three dots
following a symbol for an element that may have more than one representation,
the pattern for the simple descriptive sentence may be symbolized as:

(Topic) (A...) SV (P)

貴。	guì.	They're expensive.
書貴。	shū guì.	The books are more expensive.
很貴。	hěn guì.	They're very expensive.
書真很貴嗎？	shū, zhēn hěn guì ma?	Are books really very expensiv‹
真不很貴。	zhēn bùhěn guì.	They're really not very expensive.
書不貴嗎？	shū, búguì ma?*	Aren't books expensive?
不貴。	búguì.	No, they're not.

---

*<u>bù-</u> changes to <u>bú-</u> before a syllable carrying the fourth tone (S 1.2.9)

1.1.3.2 <u>The functive sentence</u> (S 2.6). The main word of a functive sentence is a functive verb, occurring in the comment, optionally preceded by a topic. Within the comment, the functive verb is optionally preceded by one or more modifying adverbs and optionally followed by a sentence particle, such as <u>ma</u>. Certain functive verbs are optionally followed by an object (1.1.2.4); the two functive verbs in this lesson are both of this kind. Thus:

(Topic) (A...) V (O) (P)

In the following examples, <u>yě</u> "also, too, neither" is a fixed adverb.

她看書嗎？	tā kàn shū ma?	Does she read books?
看。	kàn.	Yes, she does.
也看報嗎？	yě kàn bào ma?	Does she read newspapers, too?
也看報。	yě kàn bào.	Yes, she reads newspapers, too.
她不買報嗎？	tā bùmǎi bào ma?	Doesn't she buy newspapers?
不買。	bùmǎi.	No, she doesn't.
她也不買書嗎？	tā yě bùmǎi shū ma?	Doesn't she buy newspapers, either?
也不買書。	yě bùmǎi shū.	No, she doesn't buy books, either.

1.1.3.3 <u>The choice-type question.</u> Both the simple descriptive sentence and the functive sentence participate in choice-type question patterns involving the co-ordinate "or" relationship (1.1.2.3).

1.1.3.3.1 <u>Choose the noun topic.</u>

N_1 SV, N_2 SV? (S 1.12.1)

N_1 V O, N_2 V O? (S 2.7.2)

| 書貴，報貴？ | 'shū guì, 'bào guì? | Which are more expensive, books or newspapers? |

你看報，他　　　　'nǐ kàn bào, 'tā　　　　Which of you is reading

看報？　　　　　　　kàn bào?　　　　　　　newspapers, you or he?

1.1.3.3.2　Choose the modifying noun.

$$N_1 \text{ N SV}, N_2 \text{ N SV? (S 2.8)}$$
(Topic) V N_1 O, V N_2 o? (S 2.7.3)

中國書貴，　　　　'Zhōngguo shū guì,　　Which are more expensive,

美國書貴？　　　　'Meiguo shū guì?　　　Chinese books or American

　　　　　　　　　　　　　　　　　　　　　　ones?

你看中國報，　　　nǐ kàn 'Zhōngguo bào,　Which do you read, Chinese

看美國報？　　　　kàn 'Měiguo bào?　　　newspapers or American ones?

1.1.3.3.3　Choose the object.

(Topic) V O_1, V O_2? (S 2.7.2)

你看書，看報？　nǐ kàn shū, kàn bào?　Which do you read, books or

　　　　　　　　　　　　　　　　　　　　newspapers?

1.1.3.3.4　Choice-type questions involving negation of the verb.　In
these patterns, the negative adverb usually carries the neutral tone.

(Topic) SV bu-SV? (S 1.12.2)
(Topic) V bu-V O? (S 2.7.4.1)
(Topic) V O bu-V? (S 2.7.4.2)

中國書，貴　　　Zhōngguo shū, 'guì　　Are Chinese books expensive

不貴？　　　　　buguì?　　　　　　　　(or not)?

他看不看書？　　tā 'kàn bukàn shū?　　Does he read books (or not)?

他看書不看？　　tā kàn 'shū bukàn?　　(Same meaning.)

These patterns are extremely common in Chinese and have none of the
peremptory flavor that the English versions would have if the words in
parentheses were included.

1.2 _Writing._ Extant examples of Chinese writing date back some three and a half millennia. During this period, the writing system has been changing constantly, and there have been several standardizations promulgated at various times by the central government, most recently by the government of the People's Republic during the 1940's and 1950's. The changes have been massive, but they really amount to changes in detail, and the basic principle underlying the Chinese writing system has remained virtually the same. In the following paragraphs, this principle and some of the important practices now followed in writing Chinese characters will be described.

1.2.1 _The character and the morpheme._ The Chinese language is sometimes characterized as "monosyllabic". This characterization is reasonably accurate if it is understood to mean that most Chinese morphemes are one syllable long. Exceptions are polysyllabic morphemes, some native Chinese and many more borrowed from foreign languages; and a few common morphemes that are shorter than one syllable long.

Since the beginning, the Chinese writing system can be described as holding with rare exceptions to the principle that one syllable is written with one symbol, called a "character". In the early stages of the history of Chinese writing, morphemes with different meanings, but pronounced the same, or nearly the same, were often written with the same character. Later, means were found to distinguish a character assigned to one morpheme from another character assigned to another homophonous or nearly homophonous morpheme. Thus there evolved the refinement of the earlier principle that operates now, that every morpheme be written with a unique character. As shall become apparent in this and later lessons, there is some departure from this principle: some morphemes are written in two or more ways, and some characters represent two or more morphemes.

1.2.3 _Writing characters._ Writing is important in learning how to read. Continuous practice in writing Chinese characters provides invaluable physical reinforcement of the learning process. In practicing the writing of characters, it is important that certain conventions be learned and followed. Calligraphy is highly regarded wherever Chinese characters are used, and the proper manipulation of the Chinese writing brush, with its highly flexible tip permitting

delicate variation in the thickness of strokes, is understood by most literate
Chinese. For the present course, however, it is enough to learn just the basic
elements of how to write Chinese characters with Western-style writing imple-
ments. These elements are conveniently grouped under two headings: stroke
direction and stroke order.

1.2.3.1 <u>Stroke direction.</u> In these lessons, each character will be introduced with supplementary numbers next to each stroke, indicating the order of
the strokes, and positioned so as to suggest the direction in which the stroke
is to be made. Single strokes fall into four groups: dots, horizontals,
verticals, and combinations.

1.2.3.1.1 <u>The dot.</u> Dots are strokes of minimal but still discernible
length, and hence discernible direction. The direction of a dot is determined
by its position in a character. The details are best learned by induction,
from the stroke-order indications given when the characters are introduced.

1.2.3.1.2 <u>The horizontal.</u> Horizontal strokes are written from left to
right. There are three kinds of simple horizontals. One is slightly thicker
at the ends than it is in the middle. (The figure "1" is added to indicate
where the stroke begins.)

Another kind ends in a downward hook:

The third kind rises and ends in a point:

1.2.3.1.3 <u>The vertical.</u> Vertical strokes are written from top to bottom.
There are four kinds. The first kind ends evenly, or in a point.

The second kind ends in a hook:

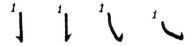

The third kind slants to the left and ends in a point:

The fourth kind slants to the right and bulges slightly before it ends in a point:

1.2.3.1.4 Combinations. Some examples of the horizontal-vertical combination:

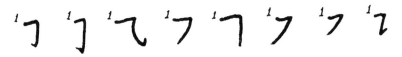

Some examples of the vertical-horizontal combination:

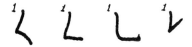

More complex combinations:

1.2.3.2 Stroke order. In characters made up of two or more strokes, strokes may cross, or they may be organized as a middle element flanked by two symmetrical outside elements; otherwise, they are free-standing. In larger characters, strokes are often conventionally recognized as forming groups, and the strokes of each group are written as a unit.

    1.2.3.2.1 <u>The order of free-standing strokes and of groups.</u> From top to bottom:

From left to right:

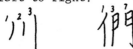

From outside to inside, except that the inside of a box precedes the last sealing stroke:

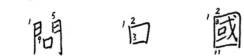

    1.2.3.2.2 <u>The order of strokes that cross.</u> In general, a horizontal stroke or group of strokes in written before the crossing vertical:

Exceptions include the horizontal stroke that rises and ends in a point: it is written last, after the crossing vertical:

The following groups are exceptional and should be learned separately:

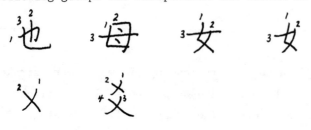

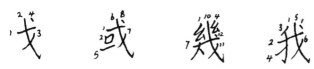

1.2.3.2.3 <u>Strokes that are organized as a middle element flanked by two</u>
<u>symmetrical outside elements.</u> When only a few strokes are involved, the
middle element is written first, then the two outside elements:

With more complicated groups, the left-to-right order may be followed:

1.2.3.3 <u>General remarks.</u> One character should follow another on the
page as though each occupied a square space. These squares should be all the
same size, no matter whether the characters occupying them are simple or
complicated. The beginner will find it useful to practice writing on paper
that has been ruled off in squares that are about a half inch on a side.
Each character should fit neatly into its square. In handwriting, it is
common practice to write horizontals with a slight slant upward to the right.

1.2.4 <u>"Radicals" and "remainders".</u> The traditional arrangement of
characters according to their shapes involved first placing them in 214 groups
whose members share a common set of strokes called a "radical". A character
is one of these radicals, or it consists of a radical plus a "remainder".
In the case of two characters in these lessons, the character is shorter than
the radical to which it has been assigned, but it is similar to the radical
in shape. Often the radical indicates the general semantic area of the word
that the character represents, and the remainder gives a hint of the sound of
the word (in which case it is sometimes called a "phonetic"); but the semantic
and phonological hints supplied by the written shapes are not reliable.

Sometimes a radical has a variant form when it appears as part of a
character, and usually this variant has fewer strokes than the radical has

when it stands alone. The radical groups are arranged in a conventional
order based on the number of strokes in the radical when it stands alone.

Within radical groups, the characters are arranged according to the
number of strokes in the remainder.

The assignment of characters to radical groups is sometimes quite arbitrary and may even vary from dictionary to dictionary. When there are two
or more groups of strokes any of which would qualify as the radical of the
character in which they appear, the student is often at a loss to decide
under which radical the character is likely to appear in his dictionary.
Also somewhat arbitrary and inconsistent is the stroke count of the remainder.

It is not the purpose of these lessons to teach the use of a Chinese
dictionary. Nevertheless, it is wise for the student to familiarize himself
with the radicals and stroke counts as he learns the characters. We provide
this information for each character when it is introduced. Under the character, we give first a number indicating the total number of strokes with
which it is written, then a code giving the number of the radical in the
traditional order and the number of strokes in the remainder, and finally we
give the radical in the form that it has when written alone. Thus:

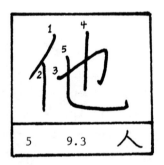

means that the character 他 has 5 strokes, that its radical is number 9 in
the traditional order of radicals, and that when it is written alone this
radical is 人 .

1.2.5 <u>Simplified characters.</u> The People's Republic has promulgated a
new orthography which has somewhat shortened the list of characters to be
used; more importantly, according to the new orthography, the number of

strokes used to write many characters has been reduced, and often the radical of the simplified form of a character is different from that of the original unsimplified form. These simplified characters are now in general use in the People's Republic, and the student who wants to read material published there must know them. We feel that the unsimplified characters are still important. A student who wants to read texts published earlier than 1949, or published after that date in the Republic of China or in other areas outside the People's Republic, must know these forms. Because it is easier to learn the simplified forms after having mastered the unsimplified forms rather than the other way around, we make the learning of the unsimplified forms the primary subject of the lessons and relegate the simplified forms to a secondary status.

New characters

國 國	看	她	也
11 31.8 口	9 109.4 目	6 38.3 女	3 5.2 乙
報 報	美	好	不
12 32.9 土	9 123.3 羊	6 38.3 女	4 1.3 一
貴 貴	們	你	中
12 154.5 貝	10 9.8 人	7 9.5 人	4 2.3 丨
買 買	書	我	太
12 154.5 貝	10 73.6 日	7 62.3 戈	4 37.1 大
嗎 嗎	真	很	他
13 30.10 口	10 109.5 目	9 60.6 彳	5 9.3 人

Variant form

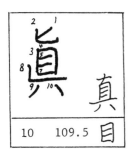

10	109.5 目

Simplified forms

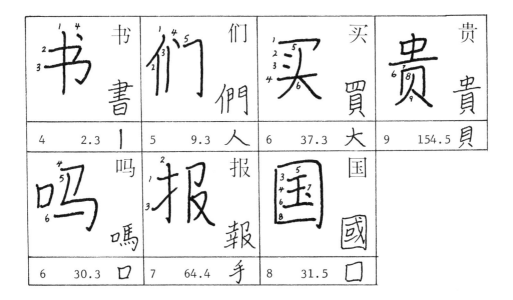

书 書	们 們	买 買	贵 貴
4 2.3 丨	5 9.3 人	6 37.3 大	9 154.5 貝
吗 嗎	报 報	国 國	
6 30.3 口	7 64.4 手	8 31.5 口	

II. New words

好	hǎo SV	good SSC 1; **well, healthy** 2
好。	hǎo. IE[1]	That will be fine.
嗎	ma P	(question particle) 1
很	hěn A	very 1
不	bù-, bú- A	not (bú- before ˋ) 1
也	yě A	also, too, either 2
我	wǒ N	I 2
們	-men BF	(added to certain nouns denoting human beings, indicates plural number) 2
你	nǐ N	you (singular) 2
他	tā N	he, she[2]
她	tā N	she[2]
買	mǎi V	buy, shop for 2
書	shū N	book 2
看	kàn V	read 2
報	bào N	newspaper 2
中	zhōng	(center)

---

[1] "IE" stands for "idiomatic expression", which is a word or expression whose grammatical characteristics or structure are for the time being left unexplained.

[2] The graphic distinction between masculine and feminine genders in the personal pronouns is recent and is probably the result of influence from Western languages.

國		guó	(nation)
	中國	Zhōngguo N	China 2
美		měi	(beautiful)
	美國	Měiguo N	America, the United States 2
貴		guì SV	expensive 2
太		tài A	too, excessively 2
真		zhēn A	truly 1

III.   Phrases and sentences

好
好。

嗎
好嗎？

很
很好嗎？

不
不好嗎？不不好嗎？很不好。很不好。

也
也好嗎？也好。也很好。也不

我
我好。我很好。

們
我們很好。我們也很好。

你
也很好嗎？你好嗎？你們好嗎？你們

他
他也很好嗎？他們也很好。

她
她好嗎？她不好嗎？她也
不很好嗎？

買
買嗎？不買嗎？你不買嗎？
我不買。

書
你買書嗎？我不買書。
她買書。

看
她看書不看？她看。她
也看書嗎？也看。

報
他買書，買報？他買報。
她也買報。你看報不
看？我看報。

中
中國。她買中國書，也買
中國報。

國
國。

美
美國。美國報好，中國

貴

太

真

報好？美國報很好，中國報也很好。

貴嗎？不貴。美國書貴不貴？很貴。

太貴嗎？中國書太貴嗎？太貴，我不買。

真好。真貴。真不很貴。美國報真不太貴。

IV. Dialogs (regular characters)

（一）

A 你們好嗎？
B 我們很好。
A 他們也好嗎？
B 他們也很好。

（二）

A 你買書不買？
B 我不買，她買。
A 她買中國書嗎？
B 她買中國書。
A 她也買美國書嗎？
B 她也買美國書。

IV. Dialogs (regular characters)

（三）

A 他看書，看報？

B 他看書，也看報。

A 他也買報嗎？

B 也買。

A 他買中國報，買美國報？

B 他買美國報，不買中國報，中國報太貴。

A 真太貴嗎？

B 真太貴。

A 我們看中國書。中國書真好，也不太貴。你們也看嗎？

B 我們也看。中國書真好。

（四）

A 你們看不看中國書？

V. <u>Dialogs (simplified characters)</u>

（一）

A 你们好吗？

B 我们很好。

A 他们也很好吗？

B 他们也很好。

（二）

A 你买书不买？

B 我不买，她买。

A 她买中国书吗？

B 她买中国书。

A 她也买美国书吗？

B 她也买美国书。

（三）

A 他看书，看报？

B 他看书，也看报。

A 他也买报吗？

B 也买。

A 他买中国报，买美国报？

B 他买美国报，不买中国
    报；中国报太贵。

A 真太贵吗？

B 真太贵。

（四）

A 你们看不看中国书？

B 我们看中国书。中国书
    真好，也不太贵。
    你们也看吗？

A 我们也看。中国书真好。

Lesson 2

(After SSC 4)

I. Preparation

2.1 Numerals (S 4.N3, S 4.N7-8). The words for the numerals from "one" to "ten" occur alone as free forms:

三   sān   three

十   shí   ten

The words for the numerals from "eleven" to "nineteen" are composed of the word for "ten" followed by one of the numerals from "one" to "nine":

十三   shísān   thirteen

The words for the decades from "twenty" to "ninety" are composed of one of the numerals from "two" to "nine" followed by the word for "ten":

三十   sānshí   thirty

The words for numerals between the decades are composed of the word for decade followed by one of the numerals from "one" to "nine":

三十三   sānshísān   thirty-three

2.2 The measuring phrase (S 3.N1). Every noun is optionally preceded by a noun phrase that modifies the noun and provides information as to specificity and/or amount or number. This phrase always includes a "M" measure as its last element (and sometimes there are two measures). Every noun is associated with one or more measures. The measure is normally preceded by a "NU" number (or a combination of numbers making up a numeral of two or more syllables), or by a "SP" specifier (S 3.N2), or both. The measuring phrase is itself a noun and sometimes substitutes for the noun it modifies. In the examples below, -běn is the measure associated with the noun shū; sān and jǐ "how many (under ten)?, a few, several (up to ten)" are numbers, and zhèi- "this" is a specifier:

幾本書？	'jĭběn shū?	How many books?[1]
幾本書	jĭběn shū	a few books[1]
三本	sānběn	three (books)
這本書	zhèiběn shū	this book
這 三本書	zhèisānběn shū	these three books
這 幾本	zhèijĭběn	these ones (books)

2.2.1 "SP" specifiers (S 3.N2), "NU" numbers (S 4.N3), "M" measures (S 3.N1), and nouns. Specifiers, numbers, measures, and nouns can now be defined in terms of their privileges of occurrence with respect to one another. A specifier is a bound form that precedes any number in a measuring phrase. A number is a free form that follows any specifier (and so far in these material a number is the same as a numeral). A measure is a bound form that follows an number or specifier in a measuring phrase. A noun is a free form that may be preceded by a modifying measuring phrase. Also included in the class "nouns" are measuring phrases that substitute for the nouns they modify; and personal pronouns, which also substitute for nouns. These latter two kinds of nouns are themselves never preceded by measuring phrases. All three kinds of nouns occur as the topic of a sentence and as the object of a functive verb.

2.2.2 Measured nouns in sentences. Measured nouns occur as topics of descriptive sentences.(S 3.3):

這本書很貴 。	zhèiběn shū hěn guì.	This book is expensive
這三本書太貴 。	zhèisānběn shū, tài guì.	These three books are too expensive.

They also occur as objects of functive verbs (S 3.4):

---

[1]A singled raised tick (') marks a syllable with special stress (loudness The presence of this special stress distinguishes 'jĭ "how many" from jĭ " a few".

她要這本書。	tā yào zhèiběn shū.	She wants this/the book.
她要這三本書	tā yào zhèisānběn zhū.	She wants these three books.

2.3 "AV" auxiliary verbs (S 4.N3). An auxiliary verb is a functive verb that takes as its object another verb or verb-object expression. Most auxiliary verbs also occur as ordinary functive verbs with just a noun in the direct object position.

他要書。	tā yào shū.	He wants a book. (yào as V)
他要買書。	ta yào mǎi shū.	He wants to buy a book.
		(yào as AV)

2.4 Topic-comment constructions as comments (S 4.2-3). Sometimes a topic is in construction with a comment that itself consists of a topic-comment construction:

中國書，你要看嗎？	Zhōngguo shū, nǐ yào kàn ma?	About the Chinese books, do you want to read them? / Do you want to read the Chinese books?

2.5 Translating the fixed adverb dōu "in all cases" (S 4.4). The English phrase "in all cases" best reflects the adverbial character of dōu, but usually a translation involving "all", "both", "any", "none", or "neither" is smoother:

我都要。	wǒ dōu yào.	I want all/both of them.
我不都要	wǒ bùdōu yào.	I don't want all/both of them.
我都不要。	wǒ dōu búyào.	I want none/neither of them.

2.6 The meaning of dōu applies to the topic, (S 4.4.1-3):

書、報都很貴。	shū, bào, dōu hěn guì.	The book and the newspaper are both expensive.

我們都要買書。 wǒmen dōu yào mǎi shū.   We all/both want to buy

                                                        newspapers.

If <u>dōu</u> is to apply to the object of a functive verb, the object must be
topicalized--moved from its place after the verb to a topic position before
the verb:

中國書，你   Zhōngguo shū, nǐ   Do you want to read all the

都要看嗎？   dōu yào kàn ma?   Chinese books?

New characters

哪	没	五	一
10 30.7 口	7 85.4 水	4 7.2 二	1 1.0 一
高	那	六	二
10 189.0 高	7 163.4 邑	4 8.2 八	2 7.0 二
這	兩	四	十
11 162.7 辵	8 11.6 入	5 31.2 口	2 24.0 十
幾	要	本	三
12 52.9 幺	9 146.3 西	5 75.1 木	3 1.2 一
都	個	有	山
12 163.9 邑	10 9.8 人	6 74.2 月	3 46.0 山

Variant forms

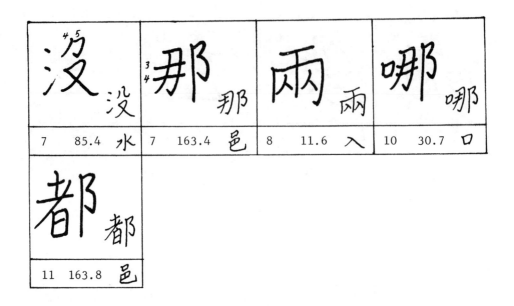

Simplified forms

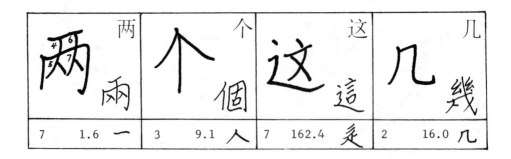

Note: the common element 言 when written by hand generally begins
with a dot. The printed form 言 often begins with a horizontal.

2.7 <u>Common radicals introduced so far.</u> When learning the characters, it is helpful to know the meanings of the most important radicals. Twelve have been encountered so far:

No. 9 人 <u>rén</u> "man, human": 他，你，們，個 。 This radical has a slightly altered form when it appears on the left-hand side of a character: 亻 . It is to be distinguished from the rare radical No. 11 入 <u>rù</u> "enter", which appears in 兩 .

No. 30 口 <u>kǒu</u> "mouth": 嗎，哪 . This radical never encloses other strokes and is thus to be distinguished from No. 31 below. It is associated with morphemes that have meanings associated with the mouth, and with syllables and morphemes that have little or no semantic content, such as syllables of words borrowed from foreign languages, and grammatical morphemes, like certain particles and suffixes.

No. 31 囗 <u>wéi</u> "enclosure" 國，四 。 This radical always encloses other strokes.

No. 32 土 <u>tǔ</u> "earth": 報 。

No. 38 女 <u>nǚ</u> "women": 她，好 。

No. 46 山 <u>shān</u> "mountain": 山 。

No. 60 彳 <u>chì</u> "step": 很 。 This radical is called "double standing man".

No. 75 木 <u>mù</u> "tree": 本 。

No. 85 水 <u>shuǐ</u> "water": 没 。 This radical is written with four strokes when it stands alone. A frequent variant is written with three strokes on the left-hand side of the character: 氵 。

No. 109 目 <u>mù</u> "eye": 看，真 。

No. 154 貝 <u>bèi</u> "cowrie shell": 貴，買 。 Cowrie shells were used as currency in the earliest times, and this radical is associated with money and barter.

No. 162 辵 <u>zhuò</u> "go": 這 。 This seven-stroke radical is nearly always abbreviated to a four-stroke variant 辶 (printed form 辶), which is further reduced to three strokes in the simplified characters: 辶 . Characters with this radical are written in the following order: first the strokes in the upper right part of the character, then the radical, in the lower left. Other characters with a similar upper-right lower-left organization are written in the reverse order: first the lower-left part, then the upper-right.

No. 163 邑 yì "city": 那，都 。 This radical is written with seven
strokes when it occurs alone. As part of another character, it nearly always
occurs in a three-stroke variant 阝 written on the right-hand side of the
characters. In this form it is sometimes known as the "right-hand ear".

II. <u>New words</u>

幾   jǐ NU   *how many (under ten)?[1] 6; a few,
                                                  several (up to ten) 4

個   -ge, -gè M   (single persons or objects) 3

十   shí NU   ten 4

十幾   shíjǐ NU   *ten plus how many? 6, ten plus
                                                  a few 4

一   yī NU   one, a, an (read <u>yí-</u> before `
                                                  and <u>-ge</u>, read <u>yì-</u> before other
                                                  tones, and read <u>yī</u> alone and
                                                  when counting) 4

二   èr NU   two (before and after <u>shí</u>, and
                                                  when counting)

兩   liǎng- NU   two (before a measure, except after
                                                  <u>shí</u>) 4

三   sān NU   three 4

四   sì NU   four 4

五   wǔ NU   five 4

六   liù NU   six 4

---

[1]Words and meanings introduced later in SSC than most of the words and
meanings of the present lesson are marked with an asterisk.

本	-běn M	(bound volumes, books) 4
這	zhèi- SP	this, these, the 3
那	nèi-SP	that, those, the, the other 3
	něi- SP	which?[2]
哪	něi- SP	which?[2]
要	yào V	want 3
	--- AV	want to 4
有	yǒu V	have 3
没	méi- A	not (instead of bù- before yǒu S 3.5) 3
高	gāo SV	high 1; tall 2
山	shān N	mountain, hill 1
都	dōu A	in all cases 4

New uses for old characters

| 好看 | hǎokàn SV | (easy to look at:) good-looking 3; *easy to read 10 |

---

[2]Some writers do not distinguish between 那 nèi- and 哪 něi-.

III.　Phrases and sentences

幾　幾個?幾個。

個

十　十個。十幾個?幾十個。

一　一個。十一個。

二　十二個。二十個。二十二個。

兩　兩個。

三　三個。三十二個。

四　四個。四十二個。十四個。

五　四十五個。十五個。五十四個。

六　六個。十六個。六十四個。

本　兩本書。五十二本書。十二本。

這　這本。買這本中國書。這兩本太貴嗎?

那　那三本書。那十二本美國書。你買那本不買?

哪　哪兩本?他看哪本?哪個好?哪個貴?

要　你要哪個?她要看那本,要看這本?

有　他有幾十本?他有二十本。我有兩本。

沒　沒有。她有書沒有?你沒有書,你不要買一本嗎?

高　他不高。他不很高。真不很高。

山

山高不高？中國山高，美國山高？

美國山，中國山，都很高。

他們都不很高。我們都要買報。

都

IV.　Dialogs (regular characters)

（一）

A　你有中國書嗎？

B　我沒有。他有。

A　他有幾本？

B　他有四本。

（二）

A　你要幾本書？

B　我要兩本書。

A　她要幾本？

B　她要五本。

A　她要中國書，要美國書？

B　她要中國書。美國書太貴。

Dialogs (regular characters)

（三）

A 你看哪本書？
B 我看這本書。
A 你不看那本嗎？
B 我不看那本。
A 她要不要看那本書？
B 她也不要看那本書。
A 她要看哪本書？
B 她也要看這本書。
A 這本書好看。

（四）

A 那本書貴不貴？
B 那本書不貴。
A 你要買幾本？
B 我要買六本。

（五）

A 那幾個山都很高嗎？
B 那個山很高。這幾個山不很高。
A 這兩個山都不很高嗎？
B 都不很高。

（六）

A 那三十二本書，你都有嗎？
B 我不都有。這十一本，我都沒有。
A 你要買幾本？
B 這十一本，我都要買。

V. Dialogs (simplified characters)

（一）

A 你有中国书吗？

B 我没有，他有。

A 他有几本？

B 他有四本。

（二）

A 你要几本书？

B 我要两本书。

A 她要几本？

B 她要五本。

A 她要中国书，要美国书？

B 她要美国书。中国书
太贵。

（三）

A 你看哪本书？

B 我看这本书。

A 你不看那本吗？

B 我不看那本。

A 她要不要看那本书？

B 她也不要看那本书。

A 她要看哪本书？

B 她也要看这本书。这本
书好看。

（四）

A 那本书贵不贵？

B 那本书不贵。

A 你要买几本？

B 我要买六本。

（五）

A 那几个山都很高吗？

B 那个山很高。这几个
　　山不很高。

A 这两个山都不很高吗？

B 都不很高。

（六）

A 那三十二本书，你都有

　　吗？

B 我不都有。这十一本，
　　我都没有。

A 你要买几本？

B 这十一本，我都要买。

Lesson 3

(After SSC 5)

I. Preparation

3.1 <u>Modification of nouns by stative verbs (S 4.5)</u>. A stative verb may directly precede the noun it modifies, especially if the stative verb is only one syllable long.

| 好書 | hǎo shū | good books |
| 高山 | gāo shān | high mountains |

3.2 <u>Surnames and titles (S 5.N1-2)</u>. The nouns <u>xiānsheng</u> "gentleman" and <u>tàitai</u> "lady" occur after surnames and function as titles:

| 高先生 | Gāo Xiānsheng | Mr. Kao |
| 張太太 | Zhāng Tàitai | Mrs. Chang |

With the exception of a very few rare two-syllable surnames, Chinese surnames are one syllable long. Two-syllable surnames are free forms, whereas one-syllable surnames are bound, occurring only before titles and given names, or after <u>xìng</u> "be surnamed":

| 他姓高。 | tā xìng Gāo. | His surname is Kao. |

3.3 <u>Content questions (S 5.8)</u>. Questions that ask for specific information are called "content questions", and are distinguished from questions with <u>ma</u> and choice type questions, which only ask for assent or dissent. Content questions have question words, such as the specifier <u>něi-</u> "which?", the number <u>jǐ</u> "how many (under ten)?", and the nouns <u>shéi</u> "who?" and <u>shémma</u> "what?" In both direct and indirect questions, the question word occupies the same position in the sentence as the word it replaces:

| 你要哪個？ | nǐ yào něige? | Which one do you want? |
| 她不說她 | tā bùshuō, tā | She isn't saying which one |

要哪個。   yào něige.   she wants.

3.4 <u>Sentences as direct objects (S 5.7)</u>. Certain verbs, such as <u>shuō</u> "say" have a sentence as their direct object. In the second example above, the sentence <u>tā yào něige</u> is the direct object of <u>shuō</u>.

3.5 <u>The pivot (S 3.6)</u>. Certain verbs, such as <u>qǐng</u> "request, invite", have as their direct object a noun which is in turn the topic of a following comment. Such an object/topic is called a "pivot". In

我請她買書。   wǒ qǐng tā mǎi   I'm asking her to buy some

                 shū.   books.

<u>tā</u> is both the direct object of <u>qǐng</u> and the topic of <u>mǎi shū</u>. In sentences like

請你買書。   qǐng nǐ mǎi shū.   (I'm) asking you to buy

                                      some books.

the verb-pivot combination <u>qǐng nǐ</u> is more smoothly translated "please", and "Please buy some books." would be a better translation.

New characters

話	是	小	七
13 149.6 言	9 72.5 日	3 42.0 小	2 1.1 一
説	甚	文	九
14 149.7 言	9 99.3 甘	4 67.0 文	2 5.1 乙
麼	英	生	人
14 200.3 麻	9 140.5 艸	5 100.0 生	2 9.0 人
誰	張	先	八
15 149.8 言	11 57.8 弓	6 10.4 儿	2 12.0 八
請	就	姓	大
15 149.8 言	12 43.9 尢	8 36.5 女	3 37.0 大

Variant forms

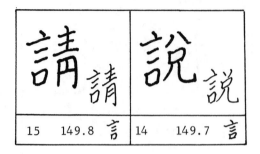

請 請	說 説
15 149.8 言	14 149.7 言

Note: the element 青 may be written 靑 , whether it occurs alone or
as part of a character. At the top of characters, `` is often printed ハ .

Simplified forms

什 什 甚	张 張	话 話	说 説
4 9.2 人	7 57.4 弓	8 149.6 言	9 149.7 言
么 幺 麼	请 請	谁 誰	英 英
3 4.2 丿	10 149.8 言	10 149.8 言	8 140.5 艸

3.6 <u>New common radicals.</u> Three more common radicals are introduced in this lesson.

No. 72 日 <u>rì</u> "sun": 是 . This radical is to be distinguished from the less common No. 73 曰 <u>yuē</u> "say": 書 . No. 72 usually appears on the left side or the top of a character; No. 73 usually appears at the bottom. There are exceptions.

No. 140 艸 <u>cǎo</u> "grass": 英 . This six-stroke radical almost always occurs in a four-stroke variant at the top of a character: ⁺⁺ . There is some individual variation as to the order in which these four strokes are written. In handwriting this radical is often made with three strokes: ⁺⁺ .

No. 149 言 <u>yán</u> "speech": 話 ， 説 ， 誰 ， 請 。 This seven-stroke radical is shortened to two strokes in simplified characters: 讠 . Most often it appears on the left side of character; sometimes it appears at the bottom.

II. New Words

七	qī NU	seven (optionally pronounced qí- before ` and -ge) 4
八	bā NU	eight (optionally pronounced bá- before ` and -ge) 4
九	jiǔ NU	nine 4
就	jiù A	only 4
人	rén N	person 5
大	dà SV	big, great 5
小	xiǎo SV	small 5
先	xiān	(beforehand, earlier)
生	shēng	(be born)
先生	xiānsheng N	gentleman; husband; Mr. 5
是	shì V	be

甚	shén	(shém- before -ma)
麼	-ma P	(interrogative suffix) 5[1]
甚麼	shémma N	what? 5
誰	shéi, *shuí N	who? whom? 5
張	Zhāng BF	Chang 5
姓	xìng N	surname 5
貴姓	guì xìng? IE	What is your (honorable) surname? 5
	--- V	be surnamed 5
說	shuō V	speak 4; say 5
話	huà N	speech, language 4
中國話	Zhōngguo huà N	Chinese (language) 4
說話	shuō huà VO	*speak 7.N13
文	wén	(literature, language)
中文	Zhōngwén N	Chinese (language) 4
英	yīng	(flower; outstanding talent)
英國	Yīngguo N	England 4
英文	Yīngwén N	England (language) 4
請	qǐng V	request, invite 3

---

[1]Some writers also use this character for the sentence particle ma, instead of 嗎 。

New uses for old characters

你好 ?		nǐ hǎo? IE	How are you? 2
X, 好不好 ?		X, 'hǎo bùhǎo? IE	How about X? 5
高		Gāo BF	Kao 5
太太		tàitai N	lady; wife; Mrs. (avoided in the People's Republic) 5
這		zhè N	this (topic only) 5
那		nà N	that (topic only) 5
國		guó N	*country, nation
	大國	dà guó	big country
		--- M	country, nation 5.N5
	哪國	něiguó N	what country?

七　七個。十七本書。七十幾個山。

八　八十個。八十五個。四十八本書。

九　九十本。九十五本書。六十九本中國書。

就　我就有九本。她就要買四本。我就要看報。

人　中國人。美國人。

大　大國。中國很大。

小　小山。那本書很小。中國不小，很大。

先

生　先生没有書。先生要買

是　書嗎？那是他太太嗎？她是哪國人？這是一本中國書。

甚

麼　甚麼？要甚麼書？她不說她要甚麼書。

誰　他是誰？誰要看書？誰要買報？

張　張先生。張太太。張先生好？

姓　貴姓？你姓甚麼？我姓高。她姓張。

說　她說甚麼？她說她姓高。

話　誰說中國話？我說中國話。他說哪國話？

IV. Dialogs (regular characters)

文 英 請

這是一本中文書。
他是英國人。他就說英文。
他要看英文報。
你要不要請他？請你說中國話，好不好？我要請他買中國報。

(一)

A：那兩個人是誰？
B：一個是高先生，一個是高太太。
A：他們要買甚麼？
B：高先生要買書。
A：他要買甚麼書？
B：他要買中國書。

(二)

A：誰是張先生？
B：我姓張。
A：張先生，你要哪兩本書？
B：我要那兩本中國書。
A：你不要這本嗎？
B：我不要這本。
A：那本美國書，你要不要？
B：我不要。他要。
A：他是誰？
B：他是高先生。
A：高先生，你好？
C：好。

（三）

A：你要請高太太買甚麼？

B：我要請她買英國報。

（四）

A：貴姓？

B：我姓張。你姓甚麼？

A：我也姓張。

（五）

A：你有幾本書？

B：我就有九本。

A：九本都很大嗎？

B：不都大。七本大，兩本小。

（六）

A：那十幾個山，大不大？

B：不都大。七個大，八個小，兩個不大也不小。

（七）

A：她說哪國話？

B：她說英文。

A：她先生也說英文嗎？

B：她先生就說中國話。

（八）

A：中國大，美國大？

B：兩個國都大。

V. <u>Dialogs (simplified characters)</u>

（一）

A　那两个人是谁？

B　一个是高先生，一个是

　　高太太。

A　他们要买什么？

B　高先生要买书。

A　他要买什么书？

B　他要买中国书。

（二）

A　谁是张先生？

B　我姓张。

A　张先生，你要哪两本书？

B　我要那两本中国书。

A　你不要这本吗？

B　我不要这本。

A　那本美国书，你要不要？

B　我不要。他要。

A　他是谁？

B　他是高先生。

A　高先生，你好？

C　好。

（三）

A　你要请高太太买什么？

B　我要请她买中国报。

（四）

A　贵姓？

B　我姓张。你姓什么？

A　我也姓张。

（五）

A　你有几本书？

B　我就有九本。

A　九本都很大吗？

B　不都大。七本大，两本小。

（八）

A　中国大，美国大？

B　两个国都很大。

（六）

A　那十几个山，大不大？

B　不都大。七个大，八个小，
　　两个不大也不小。

（七）

A　她说哪国话？

B　她说英文。

A　她先生也说英文吗？

B　她先生就说中国话。

Lesson 4

(After SSC 6)

I. Preparation

4.1 "AT" attributives (S 5.N3). An attributive is a noun-like bound form one of whose functions is to modify a following noun. nán- "male" and nǚ- "female" are attributives modifying xiānsheng "teacher" and péngyou "friend" in the following examples:

男先生 nánxiānsheng male teacher

女朋友 nǚpéngyou female friend

4.2 "VS" verbal suffixes (S 6.N17). A verbal suffix is a bound form, usually derived from a verb, added to another verb and standing in a co-ordinate relationship with it. Thus from gěi "give" is derived the verbal suffix -gei, and màigei "sell and give" takes a resultative meaning: "sell so that (something) is given to (someone), sell to".

4.3 "IO" the indirect object (S 3.8). Certain verbs, such as gěi and màigei take two objects, the "indirect object" and the "direct object" (1.1.2.4). After gěi, if both objects occur, the indirect object always precedes the direct object. The same order obtains when both objects occur after the verbal suffix -gei; it is also possible, in the case of -gei and certain other verbal suffixes, to place the direct object between the verb and the suffix.

我要給他錢。 wǒ yào gěi tā qián. I want to give him money.

你要賣給她
甚麼？ nǐ yào màigei ta
shémma? What do you want to sell her?

我要賣書給她。 wǒ yào mài shū
gei ta. I want to sell her some books.

4.4 The appositive relationship (S 4.11). Two expressions are said to be "in apposition" if one is the explanatory equivalent of the other.   In

他那個朋友   tā nèige péngyou   he, that other friend
                                               (of ours)

the expressions tā and nèige péngyou may be understood as standing in apposition one to another.

    4.5 Personal pronouns preceding phrases beginning with zhèi- or nèi-
(4.10). When a personal pronoun modifies a noun phrase beginning with zhèi-
or nèi-, it may precede the noun phrase directly.   In

你這本新書   nǐ zhèiběn xīn shū this new book of yours

nǐ modifies zhèiběn xīn shū. It can now be seen that the example in the
preceding section is ambiguous. It can mean either "he, that other friend
(of ours)" or "that friend of his".   Only context can resolve this ambiguity.

    4.6 Money and prices.

    4.6.1 Money expressions (S 6.N11). In Chinese, an amount of money is
expressed in terms of one or more number-measure phrases modifying the noun
qián "money"; the presence of qián is optional. The measures in these phrases
are -kuài "dollar", -máo "dime", and -fēn "cent". When these phrases occur in
series, the last measure may be omitted, in which case qián must also be omitte

三塊（錢）	sānkuài (qián)	three dollars
三毛（錢）	sānmáo (qián)	thirty cents
三塊三（毛（錢））	sānkuài sān(máo (qián)	three dollars and thirty cents
三塊三毛五（分（錢））	sānkuài sānmáo wǔ(fēn (qián))	three dollars and thirty-five cents

    4.6.2 Giving prices (S 6.2. S 6.4). The pattern for giving prices is:
(item priced) price (per unit or group). This pattern includes the optional
presence of one verb: either the price may be preceded by shì "be", mài "sell
for", or yào "require"; or, if the phrase telling the unit or group of items
that the money will buy is present, it may be preceded by the verb mǎi "buy".

這些書，多少 　錢一本？	zhèixiē shū, duō- 　shao qián yìběn?	How much per volume are 　these books?
五塊錢（買） 　三本。	wǔkài qián, (mǎi) 　sānběn.	Five dollars for three.
（要）一塊七 　一本。	(yào) yíkuài qī, 　yìběn.	One seventy apiece.

4.5 Lone measures (S 6.N13). The phrase yì-M "a M" is sometimes
shortened to just M after a verb.

買（一）些紙	mǎi (yì)xiē zhǐ	buy some paper

4.6 méi for méiyǒu (S 6.N19). The shorter form occurs before another
word in the same phrase, but not in choice-type questions.

他没（有）筆。	tā méi(yǒu) bǐ.	He has no pen/pencil.
你有錢没有？	nǐ yǒu 'qián méiyǒu?	Have you any money?
你有没有錢？	nǐ 'yǒu méiyǒu qián?	
我没有。	wǒ méiyǒu.	No, I haven't.

New characters

想	紙	多	女
13 61.9 心	10 120.4 糸	6 36.3 夕	3 38.0 女
新	畫	些	分
13 69.9 斤	12 120.7 田	7 7.5 二	4 18.2 刀
道	筆	男	友
13 162.9 辵	12 118.6 竹	7 102.2 田	4 29.2 又
賣	給	朋	少
15 154.8 貝	12 120.6 糸	8 74.4 月	4 42.1 小
錢	塊	知	毛
16 167.8 金	13 32.10 土	8 111.3 矢	4 82.0 毛

Simplified forms

纸 纸		画 畫		笔 筆		给 給	
7	120.4 糸	8	1.7 一	10	118.4 竹	9	120.6 糸
块 塊		道 道		卖 賣		钱 錢	
7	32.4 土	12	162.9 辵	8	37.5 大	10	167.5 金

4.7 New common radicals.

No. 18 刀 <u>dāo</u> "knife": 分 . This radical often appears in a variant form on the right-hand side of a character: 刂 .

No. 61 心 <u>xīn</u> "heart": 想 . This radical often appears in a three-stroke variant on the left-hand side of a character: 忄 .

No. 102 田 <u>tián</u> "field": 男 .

No. 118 竹 <u>zhú</u> "bamboo": 筆 .

No. 120 糸 <u>sī</u> "silk": 紙 ， 給 . When this radical appears on the right-hand side or at the bottom of a character, the last three strokes are written in the order middle, left, right: 糸 . On the left-hand side of a character, they are often written in the order left, middle, right: 糸 .

No. 167 金 <u>jīn</u> "metal": 錢 .

II. <u>New words</u>

朋	péng	(friend)
友	yǒu	(friend)
朋友	péngyou N	friend 4
男	nán- AT	male 5
男先生	nánxiánsheng N	male teacher
男朋友	nánpéngyou N	male friend
女	nǚ- AT	female 5
女先生	nǚxiānsheng N	female teacher
女朋友	nǚpéngyou N	female friend
多	duō SV	many, much 6
	--- M	plus a fraction (of the preceding measure, or <u>shí</u>) and then some 6
十多個	shíduōge	ten plus a few more
十本多	shíběnduō	ten plus a fraction of one more (volume)
	duō, duó A	to what extent?, how? 6
多麼	duōma, duóma A	to what extent?, how? 6
少	shǎo	(few)
多少	duōshao N, NU	how much?, how many? 6
些	-xiē M, NU	a few, a small amount of some 6
塊	-kuài M	(piece:) dollar 6
錢	qián N	money 6
	--- BF	*Ch'ien
毛	máo BF	Mao 5; *made of hair
	--- M	dime 6
三毛	sānmáo	thirty cents

分	-fēn M	(divide, division, tenth, hundredth:) cent 6
筆	bǐ N	writing implement 3
毛筆	*máobǐ N	(Chinese) writing brush
紙	zhǐ N	paper 6
畫	huà, huàr N	painting, picture 6
給	gěi V	give 3
	-gei VS	so that something is given to somebody, to 6
賣	mài V	sell; be for sale; sell for 6
賣給	màigei V	sell to 6
知	zhī	(know)
道	dào	(way)
知道	zhīdao V	know 5
不知道	bùzhidào	not know (N.B. tones!)
想	xiǎng V	think 6; *think of
	--- AV	have it in mind to, intend to 6
新	xīn SV	new

New uses for old characters

張	-zhāng M	(extend:) (pieces of paper, tables) 4
要	yào V	require (as payment) 6
有	yǒu V	there is 6
沒有	méiyou V	there is not 6

III. <u>Phrases and sentences</u>

朋　美國朋友。英國朋友。

友　他們是好朋友。

男　男朋友。男先生。

女　女朋友。有幾個男先生，幾個女先生？

多　書很多。中國多大？那多麼好！十多本書。

少　你要多少？多少本書？多少個？多少國？

些　這些書。那些女先生。有些山。買些書。

塊　五塊。那本書，五塊五。

錢　三塊錢。我姓錢。他說他

没有錢。六塊多錢。

毛　四毛錢一個。是八塊五毛錢一本。她是毛太太。

分　兩分錢。五分錢買一張。我就有五分錢。

筆　中國毛筆。買些英國筆。

紙　一張紙。你要買幾張紙？那些紙貴不貴？

畫　兩張畫。那張中國畫很好看。

給　誰給錢？請你給我一塊錢。這張畫，你要給誰？

賣　他賣報。你賣中國書不賣？

新　想　道　知

這張畫賣多少錢？你賣給我嗎？這張畫不賣。

你知道不知道他是誰？我不知道。

你想甚麼？我想我女朋友。

新書。新報。他那個新朋友姓甚麼？

IV. <u>Dialogs</u>

（一）

A　你想買甚麼？

B　我想買一張畫。這一張中國畫多少錢？

A　這張八十五塊錢。

B　那張多少錢？

A　那張七十塊錢。你要買幾張？

B　我就要買三張。這張多少錢？

A　這張賣六十五塊錢。

（二）

A　這張紙多少錢？

B　六毛兩分錢一張。

A　五毛錢一張，你賣不賣？

B　你要多少張？

A　我要買四十張。

（三）

A 你請她買甚麼?

B 我請她買筆。

A 甚麼筆?是毛筆嗎?

B 是毛筆。

（四）

A 你那個朋友姓甚麼?

B 他姓毛。

（五）

A 你知道你那個朋友要買甚麼嗎?

B 我知道。他要買毛筆,也要買中國紙。

（六）

A 你們有幾個男先生,幾個女先生?

B 我們有七個男先生,七個女先生。

（七）

A 他那些新筆都很好看,我不知道貴不貴?

B 都很貴。

（八）

A 這些紙賣多少錢一張?

B 五分錢一張。你要買幾張?

A 我就有兩毛錢;我要買五張。

B 你給我兩毛三分錢,我賣給你五張。

IV. Dialogs (simplified characters)

（一）

A 你想买什么？

B 我想买一张画。这一张
中国画多少钱？

A 这张八十五块钱。

B 那张多少钱？

A 那张七十块钱。你要买
几张？

B 我就要买三张。这张多少
钱？

A 这张卖六十五块铁。

（二）

A 这张纸多少钱？

B 六毛两分钱一张。

A 五毛钱一张，你卖不卖？

B 你要多少张？

A 我要买四十张。

（三）

A 你请她买什么？

B 我请她买笔。

A 什么笔？是毛笔吗？

B 是毛笔。

（四）

A 你那个朋友姓什么？

B 他姓毛。

（五）

A 你知道你那个朋友要
买什么吗？

B 我知道。他要买毛笔，
也要买中国纸。

（六）

A 你们有几个男先生，几
    个女先生？

B 我们有七个男先生，七
    个女先生。

（七）

A 他那些新笔都很好看。
    我不知道贵不贵？

B 都很贵。

（八）

A 这些纸卖多少钱一张？

B 五分钱一张。你要买几
    张？

A 我就有两毛钱；我要买
    五张。

B 你给我两毛三分钱；我
    卖给你五张。

Lesson 5

(After SSC 7)

I. Preparation

5.1 "MA" movable adverbs (S 4.N12). In 1.1.1.1, we stated that a fixed adverb always directly precedes the verb (or fixed adverb-verb combination) that it modifies. One implication of this statement is that a fixed adverb always follows a topic in the sentence. This restriction does not apply to the movable adverb, which may precede or follow the topic, with some change in emphasis. kěshi "but" is a movable adverb.

書貴，可是 　報不貴 。	shū guì, kěshi 　　bào búguì.	Books are expensive, but 　　not newspapers.
書貴，報可是 　不貴 。	shū guì, bào kěshi 　　búguì.	Books are expensive; newspapers, 　　on the other hand, are not.

5.2 "VO" verb-object construction (S 7.N13). Chinese verb-object constructions often correspond in English to lone verbs, except when the object is modified:

他喜歡看書 。	tā xǐhuan kàn shū.	He likes to read.
他喜歡看中國書 。	tā xǐhuan kàn 　Zhōngguo shū.	He likes to read Chinese 　books.

Sometimes these constructions correspond to a lone object in English:

他喜歡看報 。	tā xǐhuan kàn bào.	He likes (to read) newspapers.

5.3 The verbs wèn "ask" and wènwen "make a few inquiries of" (S 5.N12-13). wènwen is the reduplicated form of wèn. The reduplication of a verb adds an informal or casual flavor to its meaning.

wèn takes two objects: the first object is obligatory and denotes the person asked; the second object is optional and denotes the question asked:

我要問她哪個   wǒ yào wèn tā,   I want to ask her which one
　好？   'něige hǎo?   is better.
我要問她姓甚   wǒ yào wèn, tā xìng   I want to ask her what her
　麼？   shémma?   surname is.

wènwen, on the other hand sometimes occurs with no object:

我問問。   wǒ wènwen.   Let me ask.

5.4 <u>Surnames and given names (S 5.N1, S N4).</u> For all practical purposes,
there are only about fifty common Chinese surnames. On the other hand, the
list of given names is virtually infinite, and it is impossible to draw up a
short list of common given names. Usually one can tell from a given name what
the sex of the bearer is. For example, if <u>guó</u> "nation" occurs in a name, the
bearer is likely to be a man; if <u>měi</u> "beautiful" or <u>zhēn</u> "true" occurs in a
name, the bearer is likely to be a woman.

New characters

菜 菜 12 140.8 艹	做 做 11 9.9 人	字 字 6 39.3 子	水 水 4 85.0 水
會 會 13 73.9 日	問 問 11 30.8 口	事 事 8 6.7 ｜	可 可 5 30.2 口
飯 飯 13 184.4 食	喜 喜 12 30.9 口	能 能 10 130.6 肉	叫 叫 55 30.2 口
學 學 16 39.13 子	喝 喝 12 30.9 口	茶 茶 10 140.6 艹	吃 吃 6 30.3 口
歡 歡 22 76.18 欠	湯 湯 12 85.9 水	酒 酒 10 164.3 酉	名 名 6 30.3 口

Simplified forms

茶 茶 茶	问 問	汤 湯	菜 菜 菜
9 140.6 艹	6 169.3 門	6 85.3 水	11 140.8 艹
会 会 會	饭 饭 飯	学 学 學	欢 欢 歡
6 11.4 入	7 184.4 食	8 39.5 子	6 76.2 欠

5.5 New common radicals.

No. 130 <u>ròu</u> 肉 "flesh": 能 . This radical appears in its six-stroke variant alone, and sometimes when it occurs at the bottom of a character. More often it appears in a four-stroke variant, on the left-hand side of a character, or sometimes at the bottom: 月 . In modern practice, this variant is identical with No. 74 月 yuè "moon": 有 ，朋 . No. 74 is much rarer than No. 130, and often appears on the right-hand side of a character, where No. 130 never appears.

No. 184 <u>shí</u> 食 "eat": 飯   This radical counts as nine strokes in dictionaries, even though in handwriting the last three strokes are usually shortened to two.

II. <u>New words</u>

喜	xǐ	(joy)	
歡	huān	(joy)	
喜歡	xǐhuan V	like 7	
	--- AV	like to 7	
飯	fàn N	cooked rice; food; meal 7	
菜	cài N	vegetable; dish (of food) 7	
吃	chī V	eat, have...to eat 7	
吃飯	chī fàn VO	have a meal, eat; eat rice 7	
好吃	hǎochī SV	tasty 7	
做	zuò V	do; prepare (food) 7	
做飯	zuò fàn VO	cook 7	
做菜	zuò cài VO	prepare a dish (of food) 7	
事	shì N	job 7	
做事	zuò shì VO	work 7	
能	néng AV	be able to, can 7	
會	huì AV	know how to, can 7	
喝	hē V	drink, have...to drink 7	
好喝	*hǎohē SV	good to drink	
茶	chá N	tea 7	
湯	tāng N	soup 7	
水	shuǐ N	water 7	
酒	jiǔ N	wine, liquor, alcoholic beverage 7	
喝酒	hē jiǔ VO	drink (alcohol) 7	
名	míng	(given name)	

字	zì	(written character; "style" -- the name one assumed on reaching adulthood, in former times)
名字	míngzi N	name, given name 5
叫	jiào V	be named
可	kě	(really)
可是	kěshi MA	but
學	xué	(study)
學生	xuésheng N	(a <u>shēng</u> young man who studies:) student 6
男學生	nánxuésheng N	male student 6
女學生	nǚxuésheng N	female student 6
問	wèn V	ask 5
問問	wènwen V	make a few inquiries 5

New uses for old characters

買賣	mǎimai N	business, trade 7
做買賣	zuò mǎimai VO	be in business 7
很	hěn A	very much (before some functive verbs, including auxiliary verbs S 4.N11) 4
是	shì *AV	be true that 11
是不是?	'shì bushì? IE	Is that so? 7
是。	shì. IE	It is so. / Yes. 7
要	yào V	*order (e.g. a dish in a restaurant) 14

美真	Měizhēn N	Mei-chen (a given name) 5
美生	Měishēng N	Mei-sheng (a given name) 5
真真	Zhēnzhēn N	Chen-chen (a given name) 5
國先	Guóxiān N	Kuo-hsien (a given name) 5
國新	Guóxīn N	Kuo-hsin (a given name) 5

III. Phrases and sentences

喜 歡

喜歡看書。喜歡買書。喜歡
買書，不喜歡看書。喜歡
高山。喜歡看中國畫。就

飯

中國飯。這是美國飯。
中國飯。這不是中國飯，
喜歡買中國書。

菜

中國菜。美國菜。那些菜
都很貴嗎？

吃

吃飯。
吃。中國飯好吃嗎？你想
吃哪國飯？

做

你喜歡做甚麼？我喜歡做飯。
他很喜歡做買賣。

事

你喜歡做甚麼事？我不喜
歡做事。

能
他不能做事。他能做甚麼？他能賣紙。他能賣書。

會
誰會看中國書？她會看中國書。我也會看中國書。

喝
你喝哪個？我喝那個。那個好喝嗎？那個很好喝。

茶
喝茶。喝甚麼茶？喝中國茶。中國茶好喝。

湯
喜歡喝湯。他喜歡做湯嗎？中國湯，英國湯，他都喜歡做。

水
喝水不喝？他要不要喝水？他說他不要喝水。

酒
喜歡喝酒。你喜歡喝甚麼酒？我喜歡喝美國酒。

名
名字。你有中國名字嗎？

字
名字。你有中國名字？我沒有中國名字。

叫
他叫甚麼？他叫甚麼名字？他叫國新。你叫甚麼？我叫美生。

可
可是。我有中國姓，可是沒有中國名字。他可是中國姓、中國名字都沒有。

學
學生。男學生。女學生。學生都有中國名字。

問
請你問他姓甚麼？好，我問問他。

IV. Dialogs (regular characters)

（一）

A 你要喝甚麼？

B 我要喝水。

A 你不喝茶嗎？

B 你有甚麼茶？

A 我有中國茶，也有美國茶。你喝哪個？

B 我喝中國茶。

（二）

A 你們喜歡吃中國飯嗎？

B 很喜歡吃。

A 你們做不做中國飯？

B 我喜歡吃，也喜歡做；他就喜歡吃，可是不喜歡做。

（三）

A 你會不會做飯？

B 我會。

A 你會做中國飯嗎？

B 我不會做中國飯，就會做美國飯。

（四）

A 我們要幾個菜？

B 我們要兩個菜，一個湯，好不好？

（五）

B　買甚麼酒？

A　買美國酒，中國酒太貴。

（六）

A　我想他能做這個事。

B　你想他能做這個事嗎？

（七）

A　你們是多少個男學生，多少個女學生？

B　我們是十幾個男學生，二十幾個女學生。

（八）

A　你知道不知道那個女學生姓甚麼？

B　我就知道她叫甚麼名字。不知道她姓甚麼。

A　她叫甚麼名字？

B　她叫真真。我問問她姓甚麼，好不好？

（九）

A　請你問他們有茶沒有。

B　好，我問問他們…他們說沒有茶，就有水。

V. Dialogs (simplified characters)

（一）

A　你要喝什么？

B　我要喝水。

A　你不喝茶吗？

B　你有什么茶？

A　我有中国茶，也有美国茶。

　　你喝哪个？

B　我喝中国茶。

（二）

A　你们喜欢吃中国饭吗？

B　很喜欢吃。

A　你们做不做中国饭？

B　我喜欢吃，也喜欢做；他

　　就喜欢吃，可是不喜欢

　　做。

（三）

A　你会不会做饭？

B　我会。

A　你会做中国饭吗？

B　我不会做中国饭，就

　　会做美国饭。

（四）

A　我们要几个菜？

B　我们要两个菜，一个汤，

　　好不好？

（五）

A　买什么酒？

B　买美国酒，中国酒太贵。

（六）

A 你想他能做这个事吗？

B 我想他能做这个事。

（七）

A 你们是多少个男学生，
　　多少个女学生？

B 我们是十几个男学生，
　　二十几个女学生。

（八）

A 你知道不知道那个女
　　学生姓什么？

B 我就知道她叫什么名
　　字。不知道她姓什么。

A 她叫什么名字？

B 她叫真真。我问问她
　　姓什么，好不好？

（九）

A 请你问他们有茶没有。

B 我问问他们…他们说没有
　　茶，就有水。

Lesson 6

(After SSC 8)

I. Preparation

6.1 yǒu-N expressions as quasi stative verbs (S 8.N4). The verb-object expressions yǒuqián "(having money:) rich", méiqián "(not having money:) poor", and yǒumíng "(having a name:) famous", and other similar expressions with yǒu and méi, take such intensifying adverbs as hěn, tài, and zhēn, thus resembling stative verbs. Unlike true stative verbs, they do not take a certain intensifying suffix, to be introduced later. For the time being, we shall continue to call yǒu-N expressions stative verbs, and further charac-terize them as "compound".

In choice-type questions, yǒu is repeated, preceded by méi-:

她有錢没有？   tā yǒu'qián méiyǒu?   Is she rich?

6.2 Stative verbs as adverbs (S 8.4). Stative verbs whose adverbial function is introduced in this lesson are hǎo "good to" and nán "hard to":

好看	hǎokàn	good to look at, pretty
好吃	hǎochī	good to eat, tasty
好喝	hǎohē	good to drink, tasty
難做	nánzuò	hard to do, difficult
難學	nánxué	hard to learn, difficult
難寫	nánxiě	hard to write

We call these expressions "compound stative verbs", but we also point out that unlike the yǒu-N expressions mentioned above, they do take the intensify-ing suffix. See below, 12.4.

6.3 Modification of nouns (S 8.1). The modifying element precedes the noun that it modifies (1.1.2.2), and under certain conditions the particle de intervenes. The de is usually absent when the modifier is the name of a

country and is attributive, or when it is a personal pronoun denoting a
person closely related to the person denoted by the noun (S 8.1.1); or when
a specifying phrase intervenes (S 8.1.2); or when the modifier is a simple
stative verb (S 8.1.6):

中國話	Zhōngguo huà	Chinese language
我父母	wǒ fùmǔ	my parents
他那本書	tā nèiběn shū	that book of his
高山	gāo shān	high mountains

   If the modifier is the name of a country and is possessive, or if it is
a personal pronoun denoting someone not related to the person or thing denoted
by the noun, or if the modifier is a noun other than a personal pronoun
(S 8.1.3, S 8.1.5); or if it is a compound stative verb (6.1-2) or a stative
verb modified by an adverb (S 8.1.7), <u>de</u> is regularly present:

中國的畫	Zhōngguode huàr	paintings belonging to China
我的書	wǒde shū	my books
那個人的父母	nèige rén de fùmǔ	that person's parents
三塊錢的筆	sānkuài qián de bǐ	three dollars worth of pens /
		a pen worth three dollars
有錢的人	yǒuqiánde rén	rich people
難寫的字	nánxiěde zì	difficult characters
很高的山	hěn gāo de shān	very high mountains

   The modified noun may be omitted, in which case the modifier plus <u>de</u>
combination substitutes for the modified noun:

是誰的？	shì shéide?	Whose is it?
是張太太的。	shì 'Zhāng Tàitaide.	It's Mrs. Chang's.
大的	dàde	ones that are big
好吃的	hǎochīde	tasty ones

6.4 <u>AT-de expressions (S 8.3.4)</u>. In addition to the fact that one function of an attribute is to modify another noun (4.1), the other characteristic of an attribute is that it may also occur before <u>-de</u>, and, with <u>-de</u>, substitute for a modified noun:

| 男的 | nánde | one who is male, man |
| 女的 | nǚde | one who is female, woman |

6.5 <u>VO-de expressions denoting persons in an occupation or trade (S 8.2)</u>:

賣報的	màibàode	newspaper seller
賣書的	màishūde	bookseller
做飯的	zuòfànde	cook
做買賣的	zuòmǎimaide	tradesman
要飯的	yàofànde	beggar

6.6 <u>Partial inclusion (S 5.15)</u>. There is a pattern (N_1) N_2 comment$_1$ N_3 comment$_2$) where N_2 and N_3 tell what part of N_1 is being commented on. N_2 may be an indefinite phrase, like <u>yǒude (N)</u> "some (N)" and <u>yǒuren</u> "some people", or it may be an <u>NU-M</u> expression providing more specific information:

（這四個人，） (zhèisìge rén,)   (Of these four people,) one
　　一個説英文 ，yíge shuō   speaks English, (and three
　（三個説中文）○ 'Yīngwén (sānge   speak Chinese).
                  shuō 'Zhōngwén).

（這些書，） 有的 (zhèixiē shū,)   I want to read some (of these
　我要看，（有的 yǒude wǒ yào kàn,   books, and some I don't).
　我不要看）○ (yǒude wǒ búyào kàn).

N.B. If the object of a verb is to be commented on using this pattern, it must be topicalized, as in the second example above. Thus it can be seen that the meanings of N_2 and N_3 extend backward to the beginning of the sentence, like the meaning of <u>dōu</u> (2.6).

6.7 The larger numerals (S 6.N6-10). The numerals above 99 are made
with number-like measures: -bǎi "hundred", -qiān "thousand", -wàn "ten
thousand", and compounds using these measures, such as -shiwan "(ten times
ten thousand:) hundred thousand", -bǎiwàn "million", -qiānwàn "ten million",
and -wànwàn "hundred million". Those classed as measures are so classed
because they are always preceded by numbers (in the technical sense).

一百   yībǎi   one hundred

三十四萬四千   sānshísìwàn,   three hundred forty-four

                       sìqiān   thousand

New characters

愛 愛	孩 孩	百 百	千 千
13　61.9　心	9　39.6　子	6　106.1　白	3　24.1　十
萬 萬	怎 怎	姊 姊	子 子
13　140.9　艸	9　61.5　心	7　38.4　女	3　39.0　子
寫 寫	校 校	姐 姐	父 父
15　40.12　宀	10　75.6　木	8　38.5　女	4　88.0　父
親 親	教 教	妹 妹	以 以
16　147.9　見	11　66.7　攴	8　38.5　女	5　9.3　人
難 難	爲 爲	的 的	母 母
19　172.11　隹	12　87.8　爪	8　106.3　白	5　80.1　毋

Simplified forms

为 （为／爲）	愛 （爱／愛）	方 （万／萬）	写 （写／寫）
4　3.3　丶	10　87.6　爪	3　1.2　一	5　14.3　宀
亲 （亲／親）	难 （难／難）		
9　3.8　丶	10　172.2　隹		

Variant form

為 （爲）
9　86.5　火

6.8　New common radicals.

No. 40 宀 mián "roof": 寫 .

No. 66 攴 pū "rap": 教 . This radical always appears on the right-hand side of a character, and is almost always written 攵 . Compare this four-stroke variant with No. 38 女 , written in three strokes and appearing on the left-hand side or at the bottom of a character.

II. <u>New words</u>

寫		xiě V	write 8
教		jiāo V	teach 8
	教書	jiāo shū VO	teach 8
的		de P	(follows the modifier in a modifier-modified construction, where the modified element is a noun; also replaces this noun) 8
	男的	nánde N	man 8
	女的	nǚde N	woman 8
	有的	yǒude N	some 5
	有的人	yǒude rén N	some people
	有人	yǒuren N	
以		yǐ	(and with it)
	可以	kéyi AV	be permitted to, may, can, will 8
愛		ài AV	love to, be fond of 7
怎		zěn	(<u>zěm-</u> in <u>zěmma</u>)
	怎麼	zěmma A	in what way? how? 8
爲		wèi	(because)
	爲甚麼	wèishemma MA	for what reason? why 8
難		nán SV	difficult, hard 8
		--- A	difficult to, hard to 8
百		-bǎi M	hundred 6
千		-qiān M	thousand 6

萬		-wàn M	ten thousand 6
	十萬	shíwàn NU	a hundred thousand 6
	百萬	-bǎiwàn M	million 6
	千萬	-qiānwàn M	ten million 6
	萬萬	-wànwàn M	hundred million 6
父		fù	(father)
親		qīn	(relative)
	父親	fùqin N	father 8
母		mǔ	(mother)
	母親	mǔqin N	mother 8
	父母	fùmǔ N	parents 8
孩		hái	(child)
子		-zi P	(noun suffix) 5
	孩子	háizi N	child 5
	小孩子	xiǎoháizi N	child 5
	男孩子	nánháizi N	boy 5
	女孩子	nǚháizi N	girl 5
姊		jiě, zǐ	(older sister)
	姊姊	jiějie N	older sister 8
姐		jiě	(older sister)
	姐姐	jiějie N	older sister 8
	小姐	xiáojie N	young lady, Miss (avoided on the mainland) 5
妹		mèi	(younger sister)
	妹妹	mèimei N	younger sister 8
	姐／姊妹	jiěmèi N	(fellow) sister 8

姊妹　　　　　　　*zǐmèi N　　　　　　　(fellow) sister 8

校　　　　　　　　xiào　　　　　　　　　(school)

　　學校　　　　　　xuéxiào N　　　　　　school 6

New uses for old characters

學　　　　　　　　xué V　　　　　　　　study, learn 8

　　　　　　　　　-- AV　　　　　　　　study how to, learn how to 8

字　　　　　　　　zì N　　　　　　　　　(written) character, letter, word 8

　　寫字　　　　　　xiě zì VO　　　　　　write 8

這　　　　　　　　zhèm　　　　　　　　(in zhèmma)

　　這麼　　　　　　zhèmma A　　　　　　in this way 8; *to this degree,

　　　　　　　　　　　　　　　　　　　　so, such 9

那　　　　　　　　nèm　　　　　　　　　(in nèmma)

　　那麼　　　　　　nèmma A　　　　　　in that way 8; *to that degree,

　　　　　　　　　　　　　　　　　　　　so, such 9

有錢　　　　　　　yǒuqián SV　　　　　rich, wealthy 8

沒錢　　　　　　　méiqián SV　　　　　poor, impecunious 8

有名　　　　　　　yǒumíng SV　　　　　famous, well-known 8

好　　　　　　　　hǎo A　　　　　　　　good to 8

寫

寫字。寫中國字。你會不會
寫中國字？我就會寫幾個。

教

教書。教英文。教我們中國
話。誰教你們英文？高先
生教我們英文。

的

這個是你的不是？不是我
的，是她的。那本中文書是
誰的？是我朋友的。先生的
書。幾塊錢的紙。很大的
買賣。不太貴的書。有名
的人。做飯的。那個男的
是一個做飯的。那些女的，
有的教英文，有的教中文。
有人說他是一個做買賣的。

以

可以。你可以不可以教我英文？

我可以教你英文。

愛

他愛買書，可是不愛看書。
他很愛說話。

怎

怎麼？怎麼寫？不是這麼
寫，也不是那麼寫；我
不知道怎麼寫。

爲

你爲甚麼不這麼做？他爲
甚麼不吃飯？你爲甚麼
不問問他？

難

難不難？不很難。那個事，
難做不難做？不難做。

百

三百。四百。五百。五百
多。

千

兩千多個女學生。

萬

一萬多個男學生。十萬。

父 親
一百萬。兩千萬。八萬萬。千萬。
父親。她父親。她父親很喜歡她的男朋友。

母
母親。他母親很喜歡他那個女朋友。他父母都喜歡她。

孩 子
錢先生教四個孩子：一個男孩子，三個女孩子。

姊
姊姊。他姊姊叫甚麼名字？

姐
姐姐。張小姐。高小姐。

妹
妹妹。我沒有妹妹。她有幾個姊妹？

校
學校。中國學校很好嗎？美國學校，有的好，有的不好。

IV. <u>Dialogs (regular characters)</u>

(一)

A：中國話很難學嗎？

B：中國話很難學。

A：中國字難寫不難寫？

B：中國字不都難寫，有的難寫，有的不難寫。

A：你會寫哪幾個字？

B：我就會寫我的名字。

(二)

A：這個字怎麼寫？

B：這個字這麼寫。

(三)

A：他愛吃甚麼？

B：他愛吃中國菜。

A：你愛吃甚麼？

B：我也愛吃中國菜。

A：你會做不會？

B：我不會做，他會做；我就會吃。

(四)

A：你知道那張畫賣多少錢嗎？

B：我知道。九千六百塊錢。

A 你想買嗎？

B 我很想買，可是我沒有那麼多錢。

A 你想買嗎？

（五）

A 美國有多少人？

B 美國有一萬萬七千九百三十二萬三千人。

B 有二百多。

A 有多少女學生？

B 不都是。

（六）

A 你們的學校有多少學生？

B 有七百多。

A 都是男學生嗎？

（七）

A 我知道你父親有姐姐，可是我不知道他也有妹妹。

A 他有幾個妹妹？

B 他就有一個妹妹。

（八）

A 你父母有幾個孩子？

B 有六個孩子。兩個男孩子，四個女孩子。

（九）

A 你為甚麼不買那張畫?

B 那張畫太貴。那張畫賣三千五百塊錢。我就有兩千塊，我怎麼能買?

A 以不可以教我英文?

B 可以。你教我中文，我教你英文，好不好?

（十）

A 你母親做甚麼事?

B 我母親教英文。

A 她的學生都是男的嗎?

B 不都是。有的是男的，有的是女的。

（十一）

A 高小姐，我要學英文。你可

（十二）

A 我不知道為甚麼他不要賣那張畫給我。請你問問他，好不好?

B 好。

（十三）

A 錢先生很有名，可是我不知道為甚麼。

B 我也不知道為甚麼。

V. Dialogs (simplified characters)

（一）

A 中国话很难学吗？

B 中国话很难学。

A 中国字难写不难写？

B 中国字不都难写，有的
    难写，有的不难写。

A 你会写哪几个字？

B 我就会写我的名字。

（二）

A 这个字怎么写？

B 这个字这么写。

（三）

A 他爱吃什么？

B 他爱吃中国菜。

A 你爱吃什么？

B 我也爱吃中国菜。

A 你会做不会？

B 我不会做，他会做，
    我就会吃。

（四）

A 你知道那张画卖多少钱吗？

B 我知道。九千六百块钱。

A 你想买吗？

B 我很想买，可是我没有
    那么多钱。

（五）

A 美国有多少人？

B 美国有一万万七千九百
    三十二万三千人。

（六）

A 你们的学校有多少学生？

A 有七百多。

B 都是男学生吗？

A 不都是。

B 有多少女学生？

A 有二百多。

（七）

A 我知道你父亲有姊姊，可是我不知道他也有妹妹。他有几个妹妹？

B 他就有一个妹妹。

（八）

A 你父母有几个孩子？

B 有六个孩子。两个男孩子，四个女孩子。

（九）

A 你为什么不买那张画？

B 那张画太贵。那张画卖三千五百块钱。我就有两千块，我怎么能买？

（十）

A 你母亲做什么事？

B 我母亲教英文。

A 她的学生都是男的吗？

B 不都是。有的是男的，有的是女的。

（十一）

A 高小姐，我要学英文。你可以不可以教我英文？

B 可以。你教我中文，我教你英文，好不好？

（十二）

A 我不知道为什么他不要卖那张画给我。请你问问他，好不好？

B 好。

（十三）

A 钱先生很有名，可是我不知道为什么。

B 我也不知道为什么。

Lesson 7

(After SSC 9)

I. Preparation

7.1 "TW" time words (S 9.N6). A time word is a noun that tells the
"time when" the action or condition described in the sentence takes place.
Like the movable adverb, it precedes the verb and may precede or follow any
topic. xiànzài "the present, now" is a time word in the following examples:

現在她學英文。	xiànzài, tā xué Yīngwén.	At present, she's studying English.
她現在學英文。	ta xiànzài xué Yīngwén.	She's studying English now.

7.2 Follow-up questions with ne (S 5.12; S 9, p. 164). The sentence
particle ne is used in the middle of a dialog, especially after the first of
a series of questions, at the end of a follow-up question, which may be a
content question, a choice-type question, or simply a noun or noun phrase:

你要買這本書嗎?	nǐ yào mǎi zhèiběn shū ma?	Do you want to buy this book?
我要買	wǒ yào mǎi.	Yes, I do.
這幾本呢?	zhèijǐběn ne?	And what about these?
這幾本,我都 不要買。	zhèijǐběn, wo dōu búyào mǎi.	I don't want to buy any of them.
她是誰呢?	tā shì shéi ne?	And who is she?
他知道不知道呢?	ta 'zhīdao buzhidào ne?	And does he know?

7.3 <u>The verbal prefix</u> yì- (yí-) (S 9.N10). The number yì- (yí-) "one"
occurs as a verbal prefix with its meaning extended to "as soon as, once".
The verb so prefixed occurs in the first clause of a two clause pattern:
<u>yì-V$_1$, jiu V$_2$</u> "as soon as V$_1$, (then) V$_2$":

我一做飯就　　　　wǒ yízuò fàn, jiu　　　As soon as I (begin to) cook,
　想吃飯。　　　　　xiǎng chī fàn.　　　　I (begin to) think of eating.

7.4 <u>Change-of-status</u> le (S 9.N10, S 9.2). Adding the sentence particle
le to a sentence affects its meaning in one of several ways. One of these is
to emphasize the fact that the action or state denoted by the sentence is the
result of a change from a previous action or state:

書貴了。　　　　　shū guì le.　　　　　Books have gotten expensive.
現在書貴了。　　　xiànzài, shū　　　　　At present, books have
　　　　　　　　　guì le.　　　　　　　become expensive.

他一説話，我就　ta yìshuō huà, wǒ　As soon as he speaks, I'll
　知道他是誰了。jiu zhīdao, tā　　　know who it is.
　　　　　　　　shì shéi le.

Probably in an extension of this meaning, le occurs with tài:

那太貴了。　　　　nà tài guì le.　　　　That's too expensive (now).

7.5 <u>Clauses with</u> de (S 9.1). A verb, with or without a "S" subject or
"O" object may form a clause ending in de. Such a clause always precedes
any noun that it modifies. Some useful patterns are:

7.5.1 <u>S V</u> de <u>O</u> (S 9.1.1).:
我吃的飯　　　　　wǒ chī de fàn　　　　the food that I eat
他們寫的那　　　　tāmen xiě de　　　　the characters that
　些字　　　　　　nèixiē zì　　　　　　they write

7.5.2 <u>V O</u> de <u>S</u> (S 9.1.2):
説話的人　　　　　shuō huà de rén　　　people who are talking

愛喝湯的那個 學生	ài hē tāng de neige xuésheng	the student who is fond of soup

7.5.3 The clause with de substituting for the modified noun (S 9.1.4):

我吃的	wǒ chī de	what I eat
他們寫的	tāmen xiě de	what they write
說話的	shuō huà de	those who are speaking
愛喝湯的	ài hē tāng de	those fond of soup

7.5.4 The clause with de after shì "be" (S 9.1.6):

那張畫是我 要買的	nèizhāng huàr, shi wǒ yào mǎi de.	That painting is the one I want to buy.
那個人是會 做中國飯的 。	nèige rén, shi huì zuò Zhōngguo fàn de.	That person is one who knows how to cook Chinese food.

When the verb in the clause with de denotes a single action having a short and definite duration, the action is viewed as having occurred in the past:

那張畫是誰 給你的 ？	nèizhāng huàr, shi shéi gěi nǐ de?	Who (was it that) gave you that painting?
是她給我的 。	shi tā gěi wǒ de.	She did.

New characters

訴		思		弟		了	
12	149.5 言	9	61.5 心	7	57.4 弓	2	6.1 丨
意		哥		汽		牛	
13	61.9 心	10	30.7 口	7	85.4 水	4	93.0 牛
路		條		車		在	
13	157.6 足	11	75.7 木	7	159.0 車	6	32.3 土
頭		現		兒		肉	
16	181.7 頁	11	96.7 玉	8	10.6 儿	6	130.0 肉
點		魚		呢		告	
17	203.5 黑	11	195.0 魚	8	30.5 口	7	30.4 口

Variant forms

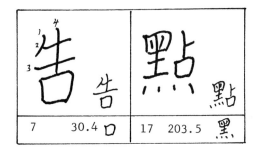

告 告	點 點
7 30.4 口	17 203.5 黑

Simplified forms

儿 儿 兒	条 条 條	现 现 現	鱼 鱼 魚
2 10.0 儿	7 75.3 木	8 96.4 玉	8 195.0 魚
诉 诉 诉	头 头 頭	点 点 點	车 车 車
7 149.5 言	5 3.4 丶	9 86.5 火	4 159.0 車

7.6 <u>New common radicals</u>

No. 93 牛 <u>niú</u> "ox" 牛   When this radical occurs on the left-hand
side of a character, the stroke order is different from that obtaining when
the radical is written alone: ₃牛 ₄牛 .

No. 96 玉 <u>yù</u> "jade": 現   This radical most often appears on the
left-hand side of a character, in a four-stroke variant: 王 .

No. 157 足 <u>zú</u> "foot": 路   This radical usually appears on the left-
hand side of a character, where it is slightly distorted: 足 .

No. 159 車 <u>chē</u> "vehicle": 車 .

No. 181 頁 <u>yè</u> "head": 頭 .

No. 195 魚 <u>yú</u> "fish": 魚

II. <u>New words</u>

哥	gē	(older brother)
哥哥	gēge N	older brother 8
弟	dì	(younger brother)
弟弟	dìdi N	younger brother 8
兒	ér	(child, son)
兒子	érzi N	son 9
女兒	nǚér N	daughter 9
	-r	(suffixal <u>-r</u>, common in Peking speech, often omitted in writing)
畫兒	huàr N	painting, picture 6
小孩兒	xiǎohár N	child 5
意	yì	(thought; intention; meaning)
思	sī	(think)
意思	yìsi N	meaning 8
有意思	yǒuyìsi SV	interesting, fun 8
没意思	méiyìsi SV	uninteresting, not fun 8

路	lù N (M: -tiáo)	road; route way 1
條	-tiáo M	(long things; roads; fishes) 3
牛	niú N (M: -tóu)	cow, ox, cattle 9
頭	-tóu M	(head: certain domestic animals, vegetables) 9
肉	ròu N	meat 7
牛肉	niúròu N	*beef 11
魚	yú N (M: -tiáo)	*fish 14
告	gào	(inform)
訴	sù	(inform)
	-su, -song	(in <u>gàosu</u>)
告訴	gàosu, gàosong V	inform, tell 7
車	chē N	vehicle, car 9
汽	qì	(gas)
汽車	qìchē N	automobile 9
點	diǎn	(dot)
一點（兒）	yìdiǎr, yìdiǎn NU-M	a little, a bit of; some 7
現	xiàn	(current, present)
在	zài	(be at)
現在	xiànzài TW	the present, now 9
呢	ne P	(at the end of a follow-up question:) And...? 5, 9
了	le P	(at the end of a sentence, indicating a change in state) 9

<u>New uses for old characters</u>

看	kàn V	look at 9; think about, have the opinion that 9
大	dà SV	old (in comparing ages of people) 9
多	duō SV	many, much 9[1]
一	yì-, yí- NU	as soon as, once 9
塊	-kuài M	piece 7
畫	huà V	draw, paint 9
畫畫(兒)	huà huàr VO	draw, paint 9
就	jiù, jiu A	then, afterwards 9
不怎麼	bùzěmma A	not so, not all that 8

---

[1] The stative verb <u>duō</u>, when modifying a noun, must be preceded by an adverb. Between <u>duō</u> and the noun it modifies, <u>de</u> is optional.

III. <u>Phrases and sentences</u>

哥　哥哥。這是我哥哥的筆。

弟　弟弟。我弟弟不怎麼愛寫字。

兒　兒子。女兒。小孩兒。畫畫兒。錢先生有三個女兒。

意　意思。我不知道這個字的意思。

思　很有意思。沒意思。

路　大路。小路。路不好。路很好。不很好的路。

條　一條路。這條路不怎麼大。

牛　有牛嗎？有牛。牛多不多？牛很多。有很多的牛。

頭　一頭牛。這一頭牛很貴，那一頭牛不很貴。

肉　牛肉。兩塊牛肉。牛肉很

魚　四條魚。這兩塊魚太大。好吃，可是也很貴。

告訴　告訴。告訴誰？告訴你父母。

車　小車。有很多的車。

汽車　汽車。大汽車。有很多很大的汽車。

點　一點兒。吃一點兒魚。我就要吃一點兒魚。

現在　現在。他們現在學甚麼？他們現在學做中國菜。

在　在。他們現在學甚麼？

呢　她們呢？她們學甚麼呢？她們學不學呢？

IV. <u>Dialogs (regular characters)</u>

A：……了。牛肉貴了。現在牛肉貴了。你一買就知道了。我看，那太貴了。

（一）

A：你有哥哥沒有？
B：沒有。我有一個弟弟。
A：他現在做甚麼事呢？
B：他做買賣。

（二）

A：英國的路都很好嗎？
B：我知道有的很好，有的不很好。

（三）

A：他們想買多少頭牛？
B：他們就想買一頭牛。

（四）

A：你那兩個小孩兒都愛吃魚嗎？
B：我兒子愛吃魚，我女兒不怎麼愛吃魚；她喜歡吃牛肉。

（五）

A：請你告訴她，我很喜歡她畫的畫兒。我一有一點兒錢，我就要買一張。

B　你沒有錢了嗎？

A　現在我的錢不多了。

B　你不是說你要買一個新汽車嗎？你沒有錢，你為甚麼要買新汽車呢？

（六）

A　張國新的那兩個孩子，哪個大？

B　兒子大。

（七）

A　你要不要看看我買的那些畫兒？

B　畫兒？那些畫兒都是你朋友錢國先畫的嗎？

A　不都是。有的是他畫的，有的是他女兒畫的。

（八）

A　你看他們那個學校很好嗎？

B　我看他們那個學校很好。

（九）

A　這個菜是你做的嗎？

B　是我做的。你要不要吃一點兒？

A 可以嗎？

B 可以。

（十）

A 這條魚多少錢？

B 四塊七。

A 那條小的呢？

B 兩塊六。

A 好。大的，小的，我都要。

（十一）

A 你知道不知道這個字的意思？

B 我不知道。我們問問張國新，好不好？

（十二）

A 你喜歡不喜歡他那個朋友？

B 我很喜歡他那個朋友。他說的那些話都很有意思。

V. <u>Dialogs (simplified characters)</u>

（一）

A 你有哥哥没有？

B 没有。我有一个弟弟。

A 他现在做什么事呢？

B 他做买卖。

（二）

A 英国的路都很好吗？

B 我知道有的很好，有的不很好。

（三）

A 他们想买多少头牛？

B 他们就想买一头牛。

（四）

A 你那两个小孩儿都爱吃鱼吗？

B 我儿子爱吃鱼；我女儿不怎么爱吃鱼；她喜欢吃牛肉。

（五）

A 请你告诉她，我很喜欢她画的画儿。我一有一点儿钱我就要买一张。

B 你没有钱了吗？

A 现在我的钱不多了。

B 你不是说你要买一个新汽车吗？你没有钱，你为什么要买新汽车呢？

（六）

A 张国新的那两个孩子，哪个大？

B 儿子大。

（七）

A 你要不要看看我买的那些画儿？

B 那些画儿都是你朋友钱国先画的吗？

A 不都是。有的是他画的，有的是他女儿画的。

（八）

A 你看他们那个学校很好
　　吗？

B 我看他们那个学校很好。

（九）

A 这个菜是你做的吗？

B 是我做的。你要不要吃
　　一点儿？

A 可以吗？

B 可以。

（十）

A 这条鱼多少钱？

B 四块七。

A 那条小的呢？

B 两块六。

A 好。大的，小的，我都要。

（十一）

A 你知道不知道这个字的
　　意思？

B 我不知道。我们问问张
　　国新，好不好？

（十二）

A 你喜欢不喜欢他那个
　　朋友？

B 我很喜欢他那个朋友。
　　他说的那些话都很
　　有意思。

Lesson 8

(After SSC 10)

I. Preparation

8.1 <u>Measurement (S 6.7)</u>. Sentences concerned with measurements of
height, distance, and length use two patterns, one for the question, one for
the answer. The question consists of one of the forms of the adverb <u>duóma</u>,
<u>duó, duōma,</u> or <u>duō</u>, followed by a stative verb. The answer consists of a
NU-M measurement expression, optionally followed by a stative verb. In either
pattern, <u>yǒu</u> is optional before the adverb or the measurement expression,
except that when certain adverbs, such as <u>jiù</u> "only", are used, <u>yǒu</u> must be
present. The topic is the object measured, and it is usually present in the
question, usually absent in the answer.

| 那條路多長？ | nèitiáo lù, duó cháng? | How long is that road? |
| 就有一英里。 | jiù yǒu yì-Yīnglǐ. | Just one English mile. |

8.2 <u>The sentence particle</u> ne <u>indicating continuing state, location, or</u>
<u>action (S 10.7.3)</u>. Sometimes the fixed adverb <u>zài</u> "be ...-ing" is present:

| 他在做飯呢。 | tā zài zuò fàn ne. | He's in the process of cooking. |

Compare:

她做甚麼？	tā zuò shémma?	What does she do?
她教書。	tā jiāo shū.	She teaches.
她做甚麼呢？	ta zuò shémma ne?	What is she doing (at the moment)?
她教書呢。	ta jiāo shū ne.	She's teaching (right now).

8.3 <u>"PW" place words (S 10.N1)</u>. A place word is a noun with certain privileges of occurrence which it shares with time words, such as occurrence after the verb <u>zài</u> "be located at". At this point in these lessons it is impossible to distinguish place words from time words in terms of privileges of occurrence. More precise definitions will appear in a later lesson, after some more new words and patterns have been introduced.

Place words, in the technical sense used here, include many, but not all, nouns denoting place. Names of cities and countries are place words, but not names of rivers, mountains, and other geographical entities. <u>xuéxiào</u> is a place word, but <u>fángzi</u> "building" is not.

8.4 <u>"L" localizers (S 10.N2)</u>. Some place words are composed of a localizer bound to another noun or to a suffix. Thus <u>qián</u> "front" is a localizer; bound to the suffix <u>-tou</u> it forms a place word <u>qiántou</u> "front". The localizer <u>lǐ</u> "inside" is peculiar in that in addition to forming place words with suffixes such as <u>-tou</u>, it also occurs carrying the neutral tone suffixed to nouns and to <u>zhè, nà-</u>, and <u>nǎ-</u>:

裏頭	lǐtou	inside
房子裏頭	fángzi lǐtou	inside the building
房子裏	fángzili	
這裏	zhèli	here
那裏	nàli	there
哪裏	náli	where?

In the Peking dialect, <u>zhèli, nàli</u>, and <u>náli</u> are regularly pronounced <u>zhèr</u>, <u>nèr</u>, and <u>nǎr</u>.

8.5 <u>"CV" co-verbs (S 10.N3)</u>. A co-verb is a functive verb which with its object directly precedes another verb and modifies it. Usually a co-verb also functions in other contexts as a main verb. <u>zài</u> "be located at" is such a co-verb.

8.6 <u>Location (S 10.1)</u>. When the location of a person or object is regarded as more important than the person or object itself, the location is

expressed as a place word, which is the object of <u>zài</u>, and <u>zài</u> may be either
a (main) functive verb (10.1.1) or a co-verb (10.1.2):

你的哥哥在	nǐde gēge zài	Where is your older brother
哪兒呢？	nǎr ne?	(at the moment)?
他在學校教	ta zài xuéxiào,	He's at school, teaching.
書呢。	jiāo shū ne.	

8.7 <u>Existence (S 10.2)</u>. When the location of a person or object is
regarded as less important than the person or object itself, the location is
expressed as a place word, which is the subject of <u>yǒu</u> "there is" or <u>méiyou</u>
"there is not":

| 哪兒有學校？ | nǎr yǒu xuéxiào? | Where is there a school? |
| 這兒沒有學校。 | zhèr, méiyou xuéxiào. | Around here, there are no schools. |

Compare:

| 學校在哪兒？ | xuéxiào zài nǎr? | Where is the school? |
| 學校不在這兒。 | xuéxiào búzài zhèr. | The school is not around here. |

8.8 <u>Place expressions as modifiers (S 10.4)</u>. There are two common
patterns. <u>PW-de N</u> "N which is at PW" (S 10.4.1):

前頭的舖子	qiántoude pùzi	stores in front
前頭那個舖子	qiántou neige pùzi	the store in front
學校前頭的那 個舖子	xuéxiào qiántou de neige pùzi	the store in front of the school

Notice that <u>de</u> is absent if the modified noun is measured and if the modifying
expression is a single place word, not itself preceded by a modifier.

<u>zài PW V (O) de N</u> "N which V (O) at PW" (S 10.4.2):

在學校教英文的 zài xuéxiào,   teachers who teach English
　先生   jiāo Yīngwén   at the school
                 de xiānsheng

The modified noun may be omitted, in which case the clause with de
substitutes for it:

前頭的   qiántoude   ones in front
在學校教英文的 zài xuéxiào,   those who teach English
                 jiāo Yīngwén de   at the school

8.9 SP-(NU-)M expressions substituting for a modified noun (S 10.5).
After a modifying clause with de, a SP-(NU-)M expression may occur substituting for a modified noun:

賣報的那個   mài bào de neige   the one selling newspapers
在學校教英文的 zài xuéxiào, jiāo   the one teaching English
　那個   Yīngwén de neige   at the school

New characters

家	法	里	北
10　40.7 宀	8　85.5 水	7　166.0 里	2　21.3 匕
師	長	京	外
10　50.7 巾	8　168.0 長	8　8.5 亠	5　36.2 夕
裏	前	念	老
13　145.7 衣	9　18.7 刀	8　61.4 心	6　125.0 老
舖	後	房	西
15　135.9 舌	9　60.6 彳	8　63.4 戶	6　146.0 西
舘	城	東	走
16　135.10 舌	10　32.7 土	8　75.4 木	7　156.0 走

Variant forms

城 城	裡 裏	鋪 舖	館 舘
9 32.6 土	13 145.7 衣	15 167.7 金	17 184.8 食

Simplified forms

东 東	长 長	后 後	师 師
5 1.4 一	4 4.3 丿	6 30.3 口	6 2.5 丨

里 裏	铺 舖	馆 舘	
7 166.0 里	12 167.7 金	11 184.8 食	

New common radicals

No. 50 jīn 巾 "kerchief": 師 .

No. 145 yī 衣 "clothing": 裏 . This radical is slightly distorted when it appears on the left-hand side of a character: 衤 . It shares a peculiarity with a very few other radicals in sometimes occurring split in a character. In the case of No. 145, when it occurs split the first two strokes are written at the top of the character, the remaining four strokes at the bottom: 衣 .

II. New words

家	jiā N	family 10
家 (兒)	-jiā(r) M	(shops, restaurants) 10
	---, -jia PW	home 10
錢家	Qiánjia PW	the Ch'ien's (home)
舖	pù	(shop)
舖子	pùzi N	shop, store 10
	(M: -jiā)	
書舖	shūpù N	bookstore 10
	(M: -jiā)	
酒舖	jiǔpù N	liquor store, wine shop 10
	(M: -jiā)	
紙舖	zhǐpù N	stationery store 10
	(M: -jiā)	
舘	guǎn	(building)
飯舘 (兒)	fànguǎr N	restaurant 10
	(M: -jiā)	
飯舘子	fànguǎnzi N	
	(M: -jiā)	

東   dōng   (east)

西   xī   (west)

　東西   dōngxi N   thing, object 10

前   qián L   front 10

　前頭   qiántou PW

後   hòu L   back 10

　後頭   hòutou PW

裏   lǐ, -li L   inside 10

　裏頭   lǐtou PW

　家裏   jiāli PW   home, family 10

　　家裏人   jiāliren N   people in the family 10

　這裏，這兒   zhèli, zhèr PW here 10

　那裏，那兒   nàli, nèr PW   there 10

　哪裏，哪兒   náli, nǎr PW   where? 10

外   wài L   outside 10

　外頭   wàitou PW

　外國   wàiguo N   foreign (country), non-Chinese

                              (country) 9

城   chéng N   city 10

　城裏頭   chéng   the area inside the city;

            lǐtou PW   downtown 10

　城裏   chéngli PW

　城外頭   chéng   the area outside the city 10

            wàitou PW

　中國城   *Zhōngguochéng N Chinatown

北   běi   (north)

京   jīng   (capital city)

　北京   Běijīng PW   Peking 10

　東京   *Dōngjīng PW   Tokyo 12

房   fáng   (building)

　房子   fángzi N   building 10

法   fà   (France)

　法國   Fàguo PW   France 5

　　法國話   Fàguo huà   French (language)

　法文   Fàwén N   French (language, literature)

念   niàn V   read, study 10

　念書   niàn shū VO   read, study, go to school 10

老   lǎo   (venerable)

師   shī   (teacher)

　老師   lǎoshī N   teacher, tutor; Mr., Mrs., Miss

　　　　　　　　　　　　　　　　　　　(referring to a teacher) 8

　　男老師   nánlǎoshī N   male teacher 8

　　女老師   nǚlǎoshī N   female teacher 8

里   -lǐ M   mile; Chinese mile (about one third of

　　　　　　　　　　　　　　　an English mile) 6

　英里   -Yīnglǐ M   English mile 6

長   cháng SV   long 1

走   zǒu   take (a route/road) 10

New uses for old characters

在   zài V   be located at 10

在家	zài jiā VO	be at home 10
	--- CV	at 10
	--- A	be...-ing 10
這兒	zhèr, -zher PW	here 10
我這兒	wǒzher PW	here by me 10
那兒	nèr, -ner PW	there 10
她那兒	tāner PW	there by her
哪／那兒	nǎr PW	where? 10
頭	-tou P	(suffixed to a localizer, forms a place word) 10
好	hǎo A	easy to 10
好走	hǎozǒu SV	easy to travel 10
	--- BF	(before an indefinite number) quite 10
好幾	hǎojǐ- NU	quite a few 10
好些	*hǎoxiē- NU	quite a few 21
少	shǎo SV	few, little (in amount)[1] 10
不少	bùshǎo SV	quite a few 10
呢	ne P	(at the end of a sentence, emphasizes the fact that the action or condition mentioned in the sentence is continuing) 10
就	jiù A	*exactly 13

---

[1]Like <u>duō</u> "many, much", <u>shǎo</u> must be preceded by an adverb, and when the A-SV phrase modifies a noun, <u>de</u> is optional between the phrase and the noun (S 10. N8).

III. <u>Phrases and sentences</u>

家
誰的家？我的家。你的家。

舖
舖子。賣書的舖子。一家書舖。好幾家書舖。酒舖。紙舖。

舘
飯舘兒。中國飯舘。飯舘在哪兒？哪兒有飯舘？

西　東
東西。好些東西。不少東西。買東西。買吃的東西。東西太貴了。東西不太貴。

前
前頭。前頭那個人。前頭那本書。在前頭。在飯舘前頭。那本書。

後
後頭。後頭那張畫。後頭那些紙。在後頭。在後頭的那家小舖子。

裏
裏頭有甚麼？裏頭有我的名字。這裏有飯舘子沒有？哪裏有好飯舘子？那裏的飯舘子很好。家裏。家裏人。你家裏人都是誰？你家裏有多少人？我家裏人不少。

外
外國。外國書舖。外頭。外頭有汽車。汽車在外頭呢。

城
城裏頭。城裏頭有中國飯舘兒。中國城裏有外

里　師老　念　法　房　京北

國飯舘嗎？城外頭呢？

北京。東京。北京路。東京路。東京大，北京大？

多英里。

長不長？那條路有多長？有一百多英里長。

房子。誰的房子？她父親的房子。房子裏。房子裏頭沒有人。

好走。這些路都好走嗎？不都好走。那條好走。我們走那條。

法國。法國人。法文。法文書貴不貴？

念書。念甚麼？念中國書。不念法文嗎？不念法文。

老師。張老師。錢老師。錢老師教我們中文。

多少里？多少英里？一百多英里。

IV. Dialogs (regular characters)

（一）

A 你看看書裏頭有沒有你的名字？

B 書裏頭沒有我的名字。

A 他要九萬七千塊錢。

B 他要多少錢？

A 他賣。

B 賣。

（二）

A 你的汽車在哪兒呢？

B 我的汽車在學校前頭的那個書舖那兒。

（三）

A 他賣不賣？

B 那個酒舖是錢先生的。

A 那個酒舖是誰的？

（四）

A 高先生買的那個房子貴不貴？

B 不貴。

A 多少錢？

B 四萬五千八百多塊錢。

（五）

A 孩子們都在哪兒呢？

B 都在家呢。

A 他們賣中國筆不賣？

A 那個紙舖在那個書舖後頭。

A 那個紙舖在哪裏？

（七）

B 不是。是那個張先生的父親。

B 是教你們英文的那個張先生嗎？

A 是張先生的。

A 那個房子是誰的？

（六）

A 都在家裏念書呢。

A 都在家裏做甚麼呢？

B 他們不賣中國筆。

B 哪個舖子賣中國筆？

B 那裏有一家賣中國東西的舖子。那個舖子賣中國筆。

A 那個舖子在哪兒？

B 那個舖子就在我們學校前頭。

B 是。我們就在那家飯舘兒後頭。

A 北京路那兒有一家很大的中國飯舘兒，是不是？

A 我家在北京路。

A 你家在哪兒？

（八）

（九）

A 法國的路都很好走嗎？

B 我知道，有的很好走。有幾條路很長。有一條有四百多英里長。

A 那個老師姓甚麼？

B 他姓張。

（十）

A 你弟弟在哪裏念書呢？

B 城外頭有一個學校。我弟弟在那裏念書。

A 他念甚麼？

B 他念法文。

A 誰教他法文？

B 在城裏頭的一個學校教書的一個老師教他。

V. Dialogs (simplified characters)

（一）

A 你看看书里头有没有你
的名字？

B 书里头没有我的名字。

（二）

A 你的汽车在哪儿呢？

B 我的汽车在学校前头
的那个书铺那儿。

（三）

A 那个酒铺是谁的？

B 那个酒铺是钱先生的。

A 他卖不卖？

B 卖。

A 他要多少钱？

B 他要九万七千块钱。

（四）

A 高先生买的那个房子贵
不贵？

B 不贵。

A 多少钱？

B 四万五千八百多块钱。

（五）

A 孩子们都在哪儿呢？

B 都在家呢。

A 都在家里做什么呢？

B 都在家里念书呢。

（六）

A 那个房子是谁的？

B 是张先生的。

A 是教你们英文的那个
张先生吗？

B 不是。是那个张先生的
父亲。

（七）

A 那个纸铺在哪里？

B 那个纸铺在那个书铺后头

A　他们卖中国笔不卖？

B　他们不卖中国笔。

A　哪个铺子卖中国笔？

B　那里有一家卖中国东西
　　　的铺子。那个铺子卖
　　　中国笔。

A　那个铺子在哪儿？

B　那个铺子就在我们学
　　　校前头。

（八）

A　你家在哪儿？

B　我家在北京路。

A　北京路那儿有一家很大
　　　的中国饭馆儿，是不是？

B　是。我们家就在那家饭
　　　馆儿后头。

（九）

A　法国的路都很好走吗？

B　我知道，有的很好走。有
　　　几条路很长。有一条有
　　　四百多英里长。

（十）

A　你弟弟在哪里念书呢？

B　城外头有一个学校。我弟
　　　弟在那里念书。

A　他念什么？

B　他念法文。

A　谁教他法文？

B　在城里头的一个学校
　　　教书的一个老师教他。

A　那个老师姓什么？

B　他姓张。

Lesson 9

(After SSC 11)

I. Preparation

9.1 <u>Imperative</u> sentences (S 6.9). Sometimes an imperative sentence is
no different from a declarative one. Usually, however, some particle or
phrase marks a sentence as imperative. qǐng nǐ... "(I) request that you... /
Please..." and X, 'hǎo buhǎo? "How about X?" are two such markers and have
already been introduced (3). In this lesson we introduce the sentence particl
<u>ba</u>, which serves to mark the sentence as imperative and to soften the tone of
the sentence.

你給我這個。　　nǐ gěi wǒ zhèige.　　You'll be giving me this

one. / Give me this one.

給我這個吧。　　gěi wǒ zhèige ba.　　Give me this one, if you

don't mind.

給我這個，　　gěi wǒ zhèige,　　How about giving me this

好不好？　　'hǎo buhǎo?　　one?

請你給我這個。qǐng nǐ gěi wǒ　　Please give me this one.

zhèige.

9.2 kuài "fast" and màn "slow" (S 11.N4). The stative verbs kuài and
màn, optionally followed by yìdiǎr "(to the extent of) a little, a bit", occu
in imperative sentences:

請你快　　qǐng nǐ kuài　　Please be a little faster. /

一點兒吧。　　yidiar ba.　　Please hurry up.

請你慢一點兒，qǐng nǐ màn yidiar, Please slow down, OK?

好不好？　　'hǎo buhǎo?

Both stative verbs also function as fixed adverbs in imperative sentences. In such sentences, <u>kuài yidiar V</u> may mean either "do the action of the verb faster" or "begin the action of the verb sooner". <u>kuài V</u> means only "begin the action of the verb sooner". <u>màn (yidiar) V</u> means only "do the action of the verb more slowly".

快一點兒寫吧。	kuài yidiar xiě ba.	Write faster, if you don't mind. / Hurry up and write, if you don't mind.
你快寫吧。	nǐ kuài xiě ba.	Hurry up and write, if you don't mind.
慢一點兒寫吧。	màn yidiar xiě ba.	Write more slowly, if you don't mind.

9.3 <u>Imminent action</u> (S 11.4-6). <u>kuài</u> "quickly, soon" and <u>jiù</u> "right away" function as fixed adverbs in declarative sentences:

他們快要吃飯了。	tamen kuài yào chī fàn le.	They're just about to eat.
他們就要吃飯了。	tāmen jiù yào chī fàn le.	They're going to eat right away.
茶快沒有了。	chá, kuài méiyǒu le.	(We'll) soon be out of tea.

The combination <u>hěn kuài</u> "very soon" acts like a movable adverb:

很快，茶就要沒有了。	hěn kuài, chá jiu yào méiyǒu le.	(We'll) be out of tea very soon.

Change-of-status <u>le</u> is obligatory after <u>kuài</u>. <u>jiù</u> without <u>le</u> expresses an even greater immediacy of the action of the verb than if the <u>le</u> were present:

他們就吃飯。	tamen jiù chī fàn.	They're eating immediately.

9.4 <u>Coming and going</u> (S 11.1). Often before the verbs lái "come" and qù "go" occur one or more CV-O phrases, where the co-verbs are zuò "by (as a means of conveyance)" (S 11.1.1), cóng "from" (S 11.1.2), and dào "to" (S 11.1.3). In sentences with more than one CV-O phrase, any dào-O phrase immediately precedes the verb.

她想坐汽車去。	tā xiǎng zuò qìchē qu.	She intends to go by car.
她想從學校來。	tā xiǎng cóng xuéxiào lai.	She intends to come from the school.
她想從學校到書舖去。	tā xiǎng cóng xuéxiào, dào shūpù qu.	She intends to go to the bookstore from the school.

9.5 <u>Purpose clauses with</u> lái <u>and</u> qù <u>(S 11.3).</u> A V or VO phrases expressing the purpose of coming or going may occur before or after lái or qù, and if after, the lái or qù may be repeated.

她到這兒來教書。	ta dào zhèr lai, jiāo shū.	She's coming here to teach.
她到這兒來教書來。	ta dào zhèr lai, jiāo shū lai.	
她到這兒教書來。	ta dào zhèr, jiāo shū lai.	

New characters

從 從	來 來	地 地	上 上
11 60.8 彳	8 9.6 人	6 32.3 土	3 1.2 一
船 船	到 到	住 住	下 下
11 137.5 舟	8 18.6 刀	7 9.5 人	3 1.2 一
慢 慢	店 店	吧 吧	方 方
14 61.11 心	8 53.5 广	7 30.4 口	4 70.0 方
樓 樓	飛 飛	坐 坐	火 火
15 75.11 木	9 183.0 飛	7 32.4 土	4 86.0 火
機 機	站 站	快 快	去 去
16 75.12 木	10 117.5 立	7 61.4 心	5 28.3 厶

<u>Variant forms</u>

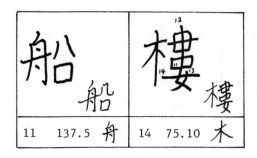

11 137.5 舟	14 75.10 木

<u>Simplified forms</u>

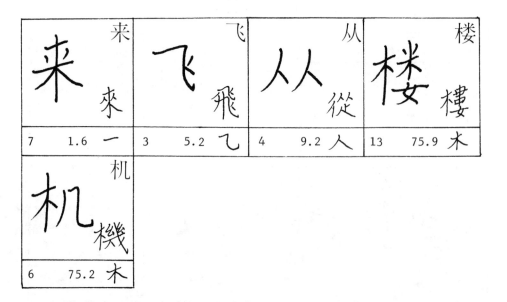

7 1.6 一	3 5.2 乙	4 9.2 人	13 75.9 木
6 75.2 木			

9.6 <u>New common radicals.</u>

No. 53 广 <u>ān</u> "roof": 店 。

No. 86 火 <u>huǒ</u> "fire": 火 。 When it occurs at the bottom of a character, this radical often has a four-dot variant: 灬

II. New words

住	zhù V	reside, live; live at 11
來	lái V	come 11
	lai P	(sentence particle, indicates motion toward the speaker) to here 11
去	qù V	go, go to 11
	qu P	(sentence particle, indicates motion away from the speaker) to there 11
到	dào V	arrive 11
	--- CV	to 11
	--- VS	so that the actor arrives at the place-word object of the verb; to 11
從	cóng CV	from 11
坐	zuò V	sit; use as a means of conveyance 11
	--- CV	by (a means of conveyance) 11
吧	ba P	(sentence particle, softens an imperative) 11
樓	lóu N	building of two or more stories 10
北京樓	*Běijīng Lóu PW	Peking House (restaurant)
	*--- BF	floor, story 10
二樓	èrlóu PW	second floor 10
店	diàn	(commercial establishment)
書店	shūdiàn N	book store 10 (M: -jiā)

酒店   jiǔdiàn N   liquor store 10

                (M: -jiā)

紙店   zhǐdiàn N   stationery store 10

                (M: -jiā)

飯店   fàndiàn N   restaurant 10

                (M: -jiā)

上   shàng,-shang L top 10

  上頭   shàngtou PW   surface, top, above 10

  報上   bàoshang PW   on the newspaper; in the newspaper 10

    報上説   bàoshang shuō it says in the newspaper

  樓上   lóushàng PW   upstairs 10

下   xià L   bottom 10

  下頭   xiàtou PW   bottom, below 10

  樓下   lóuxià PW   downstairs 10

火   huǒ   (fire)

  火車   huǒchē N   train 11

站   zhàn N   station (for trains, etc.) 11

  火車站   huǒchēzhàn PW railway station 11

  汽車站   qìchēzhàn PW   bus station 11

          --- M   station, stop 11

船   chuán N   ship 11

                (M: -tiáo)

地   dì   (earth; place)

  方   fāng   (square; direction; place)

    地方   dìfang PW   place 11; *space (available for use)

方里	-fānglǐ M	square mile 6
飛	fēi V	fly 11
飛到	fēidao V	fly to 11
機	jī	(machine)
飛機	fēijī N	airplane 11
快	kuài SV	fast, quick 11
	--- A	quickly, soon 11
很快	hěn kuài MA	very soon 11
慢	màn SV	slow 11
	--- A	slowly 11

New uses for old words

在	-zai VS	so that the actor or the recipient of the action of the verb is located at; at 10
坐在	zuòzai V	sit at 10
住在	zhùzai V	live at 11
寫在	*xiězai V	write at 20
國家	guójiā N	nation, country 11
中美	Zhōng-Měi BF	China-America (in names of establish-ments) 10
中美書店	Zhōng-Měi Shūdiàn	China-America Bookstore
中山	*Zhōngshān BF	Chung-shan (sobriquet of Sūn Wén [1866-1925], better known in English as Sun Yat-sen, Yat-sen being a representation of the Cantonese pronunciation of his style, Yìxiān)

中山路   Zhōngshān Lù   Chung-shan Road

              PW

東   *dōng L   east 16

  北京東路   Běijīng   Peking East Road

              Dōng Lù PW

西   *xī L   west 16

  北京西路   Běijīng Xī   Peking West Road

              Lù PW

北   *běi L   north 16

  中山北路   Zhōngshān   Chung-shan North Road

              Běi Lù PW

就   jiù A   right away 11

先   xiān A   first, beforehand earlier 11

要   yào AV   be about to, be going to 10

是的。   shìde. IE   It is so. / Yes. 11

III. Phrases and sentences

住
他住在哪兒？他住在學校。
他在哪兒住？他在學校住。
他住的那個房子很大。

來
他來不來？他不來。誰來？
他弟弟來。他就來。

去
誰去？他姊姊去。他妹妹
不去嗎？他妹妹也去。

到
他們到哪兒去？他們到中
美飯舘去。

從
你的朋友從哪裏來？她從
英國來。你從哪兒來？
我從學校來。

坐
我坐在哪兒？你坐在這兒。誰
坐在那兒？你母親坐在那兒。

吧
你去吧。好，我去吧。這幾個
字你寫吧。好，我寫吧。

樓
一樓。二樓。大樓。大樓前
頭。北京樓。

店
中美書店。中美飯店。紙店
後頭。酒店外頭。

上
樓上。樓上的書舖。上頭。
上頭的那本書是誰的？報上
報上說她來不來？報上
說她不來了。

下
下頭。下頭的那張紙是不
是你的？樓下。樓下有
飯舘兒。

火
火車。喜歡坐火車。很喜歡坐
火車。

站
火車站。汽車站。兩站。

船
中國船。法國船。英國船。
在美國船上做事。坐哪條船。

地 方

地方很大。地方很小。那個學校在甚麼地方?四萬方里。

飛

會飛。不會飛。能飛不能飛?不能飛。不能飛到北京去。

機

飛機。美國飛機。坐美國飛機,能不能飛到那個國家?

快

請你快一點兒寫,好不好?快寫吧。我們快要吃飯了。酒快沒有了。很快。

慢

請你慢一點兒。飛機很快。很快,酒就沒有了。慢一點兒寫吧。很慢。船很慢。

IV. <u>Dialogs (regular characters)</u>

（一）

A: 從這兒到中國去,怎麼去?

B: 你可以坐船去,也可以坐飛機去,就是不能坐火車去。

（二）

A: 你父親的朋友從甚麼地方來?

B: 他從英國來。

A: 他怎麼來?不是坐飛機來。不是坐船來嗎?

B: 不是。他坐飛機來。他說,「坐飛機快」。

（三）

A: 你們要到哪裏去?

B　我們要到中國去。

A　怎麼去？是坐船去，是坐
　　飛機去？

B　我們坐飛機去，坐船太慢。

（四）

A　你弟弟住在甚麼地方？

B　他住在學校裏。

A　你住在甚麼地方？

B　我住在學校後頭的那個
　　房子那兒。

A　幾樓？

B　三樓。

（五）

A　你要到哪兒去？

B　我要到北京西路去。

A　你是去買東西嗎？

B　是的。你也到那兒去嗎？

A　我要到北京東路去。

B　你去買甚麼？

A　我到那個書店去買一點兒紙

（六）

A　山上那些房子真好看，你知
　　道是誰的嗎？

B　有的我知道，有的我不知道。

（七）

A 火車站在哪兒？

B 火車站就在汽車站後頭。

A 哪個汽車站？

B 在中山北路的那個汽車站。

B 樓上的那些書都是我哥哥
的。樓下的那些書都是
我的。

（八）

A 你想怎麼到北京去？

B 我想先飛到東京去，從東京
飛到北京去。

（九）

A 樓上的那些書都是你的嗎？

（十）

A 我們到哪兒去吃飯？

B 中山北路有一家飯舘兒叫
北京樓。那兒的菜很好，
我們到那兒去吧。

A 好。我們到那兒去。

V. <u>Dialogs (simplified characters)</u>

（一）

A 从这儿到中国去，怎么去？

B 你可以坐船去，也可以
坐飞机去，就是不能
坐火车去。

（二）

A 你父亲的朋友从什么地
方来？

B 他从英国来。

A 他怎么来？不是坐船来吗？

B 不是。他坐飞机来。他
说，「坐飞机快」。

（三）

A 你们要到哪里去？

B 我们要到中国去。

A 怎么去？是坐船去，是坐
飞机去？

B 我们坐飞机去，坐船太慢。

（四）

A 你弟弟住在什么地方？

B 他住在学校里。

A 你住在什么地方？

B 我住在学校后头的那个
房子那儿。

A 几楼？

B 三楼。

（五）

A 你要到哪儿去？

B 我要到北京西路去。

A 你是去买东西吗？

B 是的。你也到那儿去吗？

A 我要到北京东路去。

B 你去买什么？

A 我到那个书店去买一点儿纸。

（六）

A 山上那些房子真好看，你
   知道是谁的吗？

B 有的我知道，有的我不
   知道。

（七）

A 火车站在哪儿？

B 火车站在汽车站后头。

A 哪个汽车站？

B 在中山北路的那个
   汽车站。

（八）

A 你想怎么到北京去？

B 我想先飞到东京去，从
   东京飞到北京去。

（九）

A 楼上的那些书都是你的吗？

B 楼上的那些书都是我哥
   哥的。楼下的那些书
   都是我的。

（十）

A 我们到哪儿去吃饭？

B 中山北路有一家饭馆
   叫北京楼。那儿的菜很
   好，我们到那儿去吧。

A 好。我们到那儿去吧。

Lesson 10

(After SSC 12)

I. Preparation

10.1 "C" conjunctions (S 11.N8). A conjunction is a word that connects two words or phrases that are in a co-ordinate relationship.

10.1.1 gēn "and" connects two nouns or noun phrases:

他賣報跟書。

tā mài bào He sells newspapers and
gēn shū. books.

10.1.2 "CA" conjunctive adverbs (S 13.N2). A conjunctive adverb joins sentences that are in a co-ordinate relationship. Like other adverbs, it precedes the main verb. It is different from a fixed adverb (which must follow any topic) and a movable adverb (which may precede or follow any topic) in that it must precede any topic. dìyī "firstly", dìèr "secondly", and so on, are conjunctive adverbs.

我們不走那條
路吧。第一，
那條路不好
走；第二，我們
不知道那條路
到不到我們要
去的那個地方。

wǒmen bùzǒu nèi- Let's not take that road. Firstly,
tiáo lù ba. it's not an easy road to travel;
dìyī, nèitiáo secondly, we don't know if it
lù, bùhǎozǒu; goes to the place we want to go
dìèr, wǒmen to.
bùzhidào, nèi-
tiáo lù dào búdào
wǒmen yào qù de
nèige dìfang.

10.2 dào "until" and time words (S 12.N3). The co-verb dào with a time-word object means "until", and the CV-O phrase functions as another time word.

A dào-TW phrase never occurs in construction with the verbs lái and qù, whereas a dào-PW phrase may do so.

| 她到明天還在
　紐約。 | tā dào míngtian,
　　hái zài Niǔyuē. | She'll (still) be in New York
until tomorrow. |
| 她到紐約去。 | ta dào Niǔyuē qu. | She's going to New York. |

Herein lies the difference between time words and place words.

    10.3 <u>Completed action.</u> The sentence particle <u>le</u> is used to express completed action in the past (S 12.1). The corresponding negative sentence is made with <u>méi(you)</u> (S 12.1.1), and in addition to questions ending in <u>le ma</u>, choice-type questions are made with <u>méiyǒu</u> or <u>méi-V</u>, always at the end of the sentence (S 12.1.2).

你吃飯了嗎？	nǐ chī fàn le ma?	Have you eaten yet?
你吃飯了沒有？	nǐ chī fàn le 　　méiyǒu?	
你吃飯了沒吃？	nǐ chī fàn le 　　méichī?	
我吃飯了。	wǒ chī fàn le.	Yes, I have.
我沒吃飯。	wǒ méichī fàn.	No, I haven't.
沒有。	méiyou.	

    The sentence particle <u>le</u> often occurs in conjunction with the verbal suffix <u>-le</u>, if the verb to which <u>-le</u> is suffixed has an object (S 12.3). This <u>-le</u> also expresses completed action in the past. If the verb has no object, only one <u>le</u> is present (S 12.4).

你吃了飯了嗎？	nǐ chīle fàn le ma?	Have you eaten yet?
吃了。	chī le.	Yes, I have.
他們去了。	tāmen qù le.	They have gone (there).

    When the sentence particle <u>le</u> occurs with a purpose clause using <u>lái</u> or <u>qù</u>, <u>lái</u> or <u>qù</u> must be present after the purpose clause (S 12.6).

她到學校（來） tā dào xuéxiào   She came to the school to read
看報來了。   (lai)kàn bào   some newspapers.
                lai le.

The verbal suffix -le occurs without the sentence particle le only under
certain circumstances. One of these is in the first clause of a two-clause
pattern: V_1-le O_1, jiù V_2 (O_2) (le). "After V_1 O_1, (then) V_2 (O_2)." The
whole sentence ends with the sentence particle le if the sequence takes place
in the past (S 12.71-2).

她吃了飯就走。 ta chīle fàn,   She leaves after eating.
                jiù zǒu.

她吃了飯就走了。 chīle fàn, jiù   She left after eating.
                zǒu le.

Another case where the verbal suffix -le occurs without the sentence
particle le is when the object is modified. In such a sentence, presence of
the sentence particle le adds the idea that the action of the verb has happened
to the extent indicated by the measuring phrase "up to now", or "so far" (S
12.7.3-4). In the sentences below, yíge and wǒ yào chī de modify cài.

她做了一個菜。   ta zuòle yíge cài.   She has cooked one dish.

她做了一個菜了。 zuòle yíge cài   So far, she has cooked one dish.
                le.

她做了我要吃   ta zuòle wǒ yào   She has cooked some dishes that
的菜。   chī de cài.   I want to eat.

10.4 Follow-up sentences with shi...de expressing past action (S 12.10).
There is a pattern shi X V de (O) "It was under the circumstances denoted by
X that the action of the verb took place" used after the beginning of a dialog.
shi is sometimes omitted in positive sentences.

你到甚麼地方   nǐ dào shémma   Where did you go? / Where have
去了？   dìfang qu le?   you been?

我到城裏頭去了。	wo dào chéng- litou qu le.	I went to the shopping district.
你是去做甚麼 　去的？	nǐ shi qù zuò shémma qu de?	To do what?
我是去買書 　去的。	wǒ shi qù mǎi shū qu de.	To buy books.
你買了書就做甚 　麼了？	nǐ mǎile shū, jiù **zuò** shémma le?	What did you do after you bought books.
吃飯去了。	chī **fàn** qu le.	I went to eat.
你是跟誰吃的 　飯？	nǐ shi gēn shéi chī de fàn?	Whom did you eat with?
我是跟一個朋友 　吃的飯。	wǒ shi gēn yige péngyou chī de fàn.	I ate with a friend.

141

New characters

開	氣	所	今
12 169.4 門	10 84.6 气	8 63.4 戶	4 9.2 人
跟	紐	明	午
13 157.6 足	10 120.4 糸	8 72.4 日	4 24.2 十
電	晚	雨	天
13 173.5 雨	11 72.7 日	8 173.0 雨	4 37.1 大
課	第	屋	打
15 149.8 言	11 118.5 竹	9 44.6 尸	5 64.2 手
還	街	約	早
17 162.13 辵	12 144.6 行	9 120.3 糸	6 72.2 日

Variant form

Simplified forms

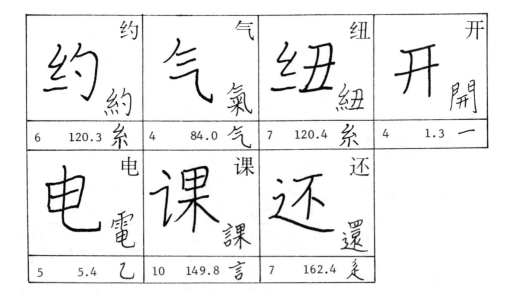

10.5 <u>More important radicals.</u>

No. 37 大 <u>dà</u> "big": 太，大，天．

No. 64 手 <u>shǒu</u> "hand": 打 ． This radical has a three-stroke variant when it appears on the left-hand side of a character: 扌．

No. 169 門 <u>mén</u> "gate": 開

No. 173 雨 <u>yǔ</u> "rain": 雨，電．

II. New words

紐	niǔ	(button)
約	yuē	(appointment)
紐約	Niǔyuē	New York 10
早	zǎo SV	early 2
早上	zǎoshang TW	morning 12
早飯	zǎofàn N	breakfast 12
晚	wǎn	(late)
晚上	wǎnshang TW	evening 12
晚飯	wǎnfàn N	supper 12
第	dì- SP	(ordinalizing prefix) 10
第一個人	dìyíge rén	the first person
第二個孩子	dìèrge háizi	the second child
第一	dìyī CA	firstly 12
第二	dìèr CA	secondly 12
天	-tiān M	day 11
兩天	liǎngtiān	two days
第二天	dìèrtiān TW	the second day, the next day 11
氣	qì	(vapor)
天氣	tiānqi N	weather

今		jīn	(now)
	今天	jīntian TW	today 11
明		míng	(bright)
	明天	míngtian TW	tomorrow 11
午		wǔ	(noon)
	上午	shàngwu TW	morning 11
	下午	xiàwu TW	afternoon 11
	中午	zhōngwu TW	noon 11
	午飯	*wǔfàn N	noon meal, lunch
雨		yǔ N	rain 12
	下雨	xià yǔ VO	to rain 12
課		kè N	class 12
	上課	shàng kè VO	go to class 12
	下課	xià kè VO	get out of class 12
		--- *M	lesson 15
	第十課	dìshíkè	the tenth lesson
屋		wū	(room)
	屋子	wūzi N	room 11
街		jiē N	street 11
		(M: -tiáo)	
	街上	jiēshang PW	on the street; shopping district 11
所（兒）		-suǒ, -suǒr M	(place:) (buildings) 10
電		diàn	(electricity)
	電話	diànhuà N	telephone 12
	電車	*diànchē N	trolley car 14

打	dǎ	(hit)	
打電話	dǎ diànhuà VO	make a telephone call 12	
打字	*dǎ zì VO	write on a typewriter, type	
打字機	*dǎzìjī N	typewriter	
開	kāi V	(open:) drive 10; start away 11	
	--- *CV	driving, by 17	
開車	kāi chē VO	drive(ing) (a car) 10, 17	
跟	gēn CV	(heel:) with, accompanying 12	
	---	and 11	
還	hái A	still, furthermore 9	
還沒有（有）	hái méi(you)	have not...yet, still not... 12	
---呢	...ne		

New uses for old characters

走	zǒu V	depart 12	
一塊兒	yíkuàr PW	one place 12	
在一塊兒	zài yíkuàr	CV O	together 12
	CV O		
	--- A	together 12	
大學	dàxué PW	university 12	
北京大學	Běijīng	Peking University 12	
	Dàxué PW		
北大	Běi Dà PW	Peking U. 12	
東京大學	Dōngjīng	Tokyo University 12	
	Dàxué PW		
東大	Dōng Dà PW	Tokyo U. 12	

會	huǐ	(moment)
一會（兒）	yìhuěr, yìhuǐ TW	a little while, a moment 12
中飯	zhōngfàn N	lunch 12
頭	tóu- SP	the first... 10
頭一個人	tóuyíge rén	the first person
頭兩個孩子	tóuliǎngge háizi	the first two children
到	dào CV	until 12
看	kàn V	visit, see (a person) 11
了	-le VS	(completed action) 12
	--- P	(sentence particle, indicates action completed in the past, having occurred as of the present) 12
沒（有）	méi(you) A	(negates completed action sentences) 12
怎麼	zěmma MA	how come? 10

III. Phrases and sentences

紐
紐約。到紐約去了。到紐約去
買東西去了。

約
紐約。到紐約去了。到紐約去
看中國報。

早
張小姐，早。早上。早飯。吃了
早飯了沒有？早上看報。

晚
晚上。晚飯。晚上吃中國飯。
從早上到晚上沒吃飯。

第
第一。第七百六十八。第二本書。
一天。第二天。頭兩天。頭一天
做事。

氣
天氣。天氣很好。紐約的天
氣很好嗎？

今
今天。今天早上。今天晚上
看報。

明
明天。明天早上。明天早
上看甚麼報？明天早上
看中國報。

午
上午。中午。中午吃中飯。
下午。他們明天上午來，
下午走。我們明天下午在
一塊兒念書，好不好？

雨
下雨。今天下雨不下雨？
今天早上下雨。今天晚
上不下雨。

課
上課。下課。第幾課？這
是第幾課？這是第十
課。頭十課不很難。

屋
屋子。屋子很大。屋子裏

頭。屋子裏就有兩個人。屋子前頭。屋子後頭。屋子後頭那個小汽車是誰的?

可是不會開汽車。

跟 這本書跟那本書。這本書跟那本書我都要買。我跟你去吧。我不跟他説話了。就有茶跟水。

街 街上。到街上去買東西去了。大街。小街。第四十二街。那條街很大。

還 我還想買一本書。還沒走呢。還沒到呢。

所 那所房子。那所房子前頭。那所房子前頭有一家書舖。

電 電話。電車。

打 打電話。打字。我不會打字。打字機。那些打字機都很貴。

開 開汽車。他説他會開飛機,

IV. Longer passages (regular characters)

（一）

A 屋子裏那幾個人是誰？

B 一個是我母親，一個是我姊姊，一個是我姊姊的朋友。

（二）

A 你今天下午沒課了嗎？

B 沒課了。我上的課都在上午。

（三）

A 你們現在念第幾課了？

B 第十一課。

A 難不難？

B 不太難。

（四）

A 你會打字不會？

B 我不會，我很想學。

（五）

A 他們來不來？

B 他說今天晚上下雨，他們不來了。

（六）

A 你們先走吧。我還要買一些東西。

B 今天下午買，可以不可以？

A 下午人太多，我想我現在買吧。

（七）

A　你父母來了沒有？

B　沒有。我父親說，他們明天坐飛機來。

A　為甚麼你不坐飛機呢？

B　有人告訴我今天沒有飛機到紐約去。

A　為甚麼？

B　天氣不好。

（八）

A　今天晚上有人請你吃飯，你知道嗎？

B　我知道。他不是也請了你了嗎？

A　是。他也請了我了。

B　你要不要跟我們一塊兒去？

A　那很好。我們一塊兒去吧。

B　請我們吃飯的那個人是誰，你知道嗎？

A　我就知道他姓高，我不知道他的名字。

（九）

（十）

A　我們想一會兒去看看張國先。你去不去？

B　你們去吧，我還沒吃早飯呢。

（十一）

A 這是甚麼？

B 這是我們學校買的打字機。

A 怎麼這個打字機這麼大？

B 這是中文打字機。中文打字機都這麼大。

A

B 還沒呢。

A 你現在打吧，他現在在家。

B 好，我現在打。

（十二）

A 今天的天氣真好，我們想開車到紐約去，你們去不去？

B 我可以去，可是國新不能去。

A

（十三）

A 你打了電話了嗎？

（十四）

有人問我喜歡坐飛機，喜歡坐船。我說，我喜歡坐船。他問我，「爲甚麼？」我說，「船很大，飛機太小。船上有很多地方我可以去。我可以在船上的酒舖裏喝酒，在船上的飯館裏吃飯，也可以在船上的舖子裏買東西。」

（十五）

A　你今天上午做甚麼了？

B　我到學校去了。

A　你是去做甚麼去的？

B　我去學開汽車去了。

A　你跟誰學的？

B　我是跟教我們法文的那個老師學的。

A　你是在哪兒學的？

B　我在學校後頭那兒學的。

（十六）

A　你哥哥買的那所房子是哪一所？

B　是學校前頭的那所。

V. Longer passages (simplified characters)

（一）

A 屋子里那几个人是谁？

B 一个是我母亲，一个是我姊姊，一个是我姊姊的朋友。

（二）

A 你今天下午没课了吗？

B 没课了。我上的课都在上午。

（三）

A 你们现在念第几课了？

B 第十一课。

A 难不难？

B 不太难。

（四）

A 你会打字不会？

B 我不会，我很想学。

（五）

A 他说他们来不来？

B 他说今天晚上下雨，他们不来了。

（六）

A 你们先走吧，我还要买一些东西。

B 今天下午买，可以不可以？

A 下午人太多，我想我现在买吧。

（七）

A 你父母来了没有？

B 没有。我父亲说，他们明天坐飞机来。

（八）

A 今天晚上有人请你吃饭，你知道吗？

B 我知道。他不是也请了你
　　了吗？

A 是。他也请了我了。

B 你要不要跟我们一块儿去？

A 那很好。我们一块儿去吧。

B 请我们吃饭的人是谁，你
　　知道吗？

A 我就知道他姓高，我不
　　知道他的名字。

（九）

A 为什么你不坐飞机呢？

B 有人告诉我今天没有飞
　　机到纽约去。

A 为什么？

B 天气不好。

（十）

A 我们想一会儿去看看张
　　国先。你去不去？

B 你们去吧。我还没吃早
　　饭呢。

（十一）

A 这是什么？

B 这是我们学校买的打字机。

A 怎么这个打字机这么大？

B 这个是中文打字机。中文
　　打字机都这么大。

（十二）

A 今天的天气真好，我们想
　　开车到纽约去，你们去
　　不去？

B 我可以去，可是国新
　　不能去。

（十三）

A 你打了电话了吗？

B 还没呢。

A 你现在打吧，他现在在家

B 好，我现在打。

（十四）

有人问我喜欢坐飞机，
喜欢坐船。我说，我喜欢坐
船。他问我，「为什么?」我说，
「船很大，飞机太小。船上
有很多地方我可以去。我可
以在船上的酒铺里喝酒，
在船上的饭馆里吃饭，也
可以在船上的铺子里买东
西。」

（十五）

A 你今天上午做什么了?

B 我到学校去了。

A 你是去做什么去的?

B 我去学开气车去了。

A 你跟谁学的?

B 我是跟教我们法文的那个
　　老师学的。

A 你是在哪儿学的?

B 我是在学校后头那儿学的。

（十六）

你哥哥买的那所房子是
　　哪一所?

是学校前头的那所。

Lesson 11

(After SSC 13)

I. Preparation

11.1 (yàoshi) X, (jiù) Y "If X, (then) Y (S 13.N3). In Chinese, the protasis always precedes the apodosis.

（要是）她去，我 (yàoshi) tā qù,   I won't go if she goes.
（就）不去。   wǒ (jiù) búqù.

11.2 <u>Time names (S 13.4)</u>. Sentences identifying particular times have the pattern TW$_1$ (shì)/búshi TW$_2$. Notice that <u>shì</u> "be" is optional in positive sentences, required in negative ones.

今天（是）   jīntian, (shi)   What day of the week is it today?
禮拜幾？   lǐbàijǐ?

不是禮拜天嗎？ búshi lǐbàitiān ma? Isn't it Sunday?

11.3 <u>Time when and time within which (S 13.1)</u>. A time expression (a simple time word, a time word modified by a phrase or a clause, or a NU-M phrase denoting an amount of time) occurring before the main verb of a positive sentence tells the time when the action of the verb takes place. In a negative sentence, it tells the period of time within which the action of the verb failed to take place.

她禮拜天   tā lǐbàitiān   Does she teach on Sunday?
教書嗎？   jiāo shū ma?

她禮拜天   tā lǐbàitiān,   She doesn't teach on Sunday.
不教書。   bùjiāo shū.

這三天我   zhèisāntiān, wǒ   I haven't worked for the
沒做事。   méizuò shì.   last three days.

11.4 <u>Time spent</u>. After such verbs as <u>lái, qù, zǒu,</u> and <u>zhù</u> a time expression may occur denoting the duration of the action of the verb (S 13.3).

他（要）來 兩天。	tā (yào) lái liǎngtiān.	He'll be here for two days.
他來了兩天。	tā láile liǎng- tiān.	He's been here for two days.
他來了兩天了。	tā láile liǎng- tiān le.	He's been here for two days, so far.

Such a time expression, optionally followed by <u>de</u>, may also occur between a transitive verb and its object (S 13.2).

她（要）開兩天 （的）車。	tā (yào) kāi liǎngtiān(de) chē.	She's going to drive for two days.
她開了兩天(的) 車。	tā kāile liǎng- tiān(de) chē.	She's driven for two days.
她開了兩天(的) 車了。	tā kāile liǎng- tiān(de) chē le.	She's driven for two days, so far.

11.5 <u>The whole before the part (S 13.5)</u>. In identifying times and places, the word denoting the larger entity always precedes the word denoting the smaller one.

紐約，第四十 街	Niǔyuē, Dìsìshí Jiē	40th Street, New York
一九三一年，十 二月	yī-jiǔ-sān-yī- nián, shíèryuè	December, 1931

11.6 *V-yi-V <u>"do an action of the verb" (S 14.5)</u>. Certain verbs may be reduplicated. Between the two halves of the reduplicated form <u>yī</u> "one" may

occur, in which case the meaning is "do an action of the verb". This meaning
is often reinforced by adding the fixed adverb zài "again".

再看一看 。   zài kànyikàn.   Look at it once more.

With the tone on the repeated syllable changed to the neutral tone, and
with yi optional, the meaning is weakened to the casual sense mentioned above,
5.3.

請你看（一）看 。 qǐng nǐ kàn(yi)-   Please take a look.

                              kan.

To indicate completed action, le is inserted:

我看了一看 。   wǒ kànleyikàn.   I took another look at it.

他看了看我 。   tā kànlekan wǒ.   He took a look at me.

11.7 Equal comparison (S 13.6). There is a pattern expressing equal
comparison: X (méi)yǒu Y nemma/zhemma SV "X is (not) as SV as Y".

汽車没有火車   qìchē, méiyou   An automobile is not as fast
　那麽快 。   huǒchē nemma   as a train.

                              kuài.

New characters

過	拜	年	月
13 162.9 辶	9 64.5 手	6 51.7 干	4 74.0 月
影	昨	別	再
15 59.12 彡	9 72.5 日	7 18.5 刀	6 13.4 冂
興	候	每	同
16 134.10 臼	10 9.8 人	7 80.3 毋	6 30.3 口
豬	時	定	回
16 152.9 豕	10 72.6 日	8 40.5 宀	6 31.3 囗
禮	夠	玩	因
18 113.13 示	11 36.8 夕	8 96.4 玉	6 31.3 囗

Variant forms

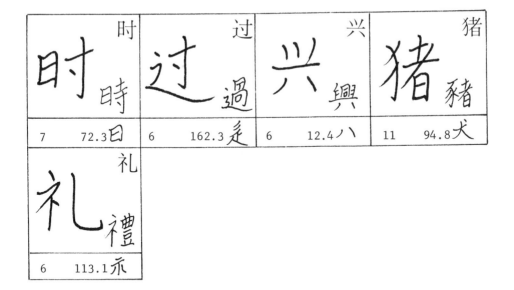

Simplified forms

11.7 <u>An important radical.</u>

No. 113 示 <u>shì</u> "show": 禮 . When it appears on the left-hand side of a character, this radical is sometimes slightly distorted: 礻 . Characters with this radical often represent words whose meanings have to do with ritual, **worship**, and the supernatural.

II. <u>New words</u>

年	-nián M	year 12	
一九四九年	yī-jiǔ-sì- jiǔ-nián	(the year) 1949	
今年	jīnnian TW	this year 13	
明年	míngnian TW	next year 13	
去年	qùnian TW	last year 13	
前年	qiánnian TW	year before last 13	
大前年	dàqiánnian TW	three years ago 13	
後年	hòunian TW	year after next 13	
大後年	dàhòunian TW	three years from now 13	
年年	*niánnián A	every year 21.2.3	
月	yuè N	month 13	
上（個）月	shàng(ge)- yuè TW	last month 13	
下（個）月	xià(ge)yuè TW	next month 13	
	--- M	(in names of months) 13	
一月	yīyuè, yíyuè TW	January 13	
二月	èryuè TW	February 13	
十二月	shíèryuè TW	December 13	

時		shí		(time)
候		hòu		(period)
時候（兒）		shíhou(r)	TW	time 12
x 的時候（兒）		X de shi-hou(r)	TW	when X 12
有（的）時候（兒）		yǒu(de) shí-hou(r)	TW	sometimes
那個時候（兒）		nèige shí-hou(r)	TW	that time (in the past)
昨		zuó		(yesterday)
昨天		zuótian	TW	yesterday 12
禮		lǐ		(propriety)
拜		bài		(do obeisance)
禮拜		lǐbài	TW	(worship:) week 13
下（個）禮拜		xià(ge)-lǐbài	TW	next week 13
上（個）禮拜		shàng(ge)-lǐbài	TW	last week 13
禮拜一		lǐbàiyī	TW	Monday 13
禮拜二		lǐbàièr	TW	Tuesday 13
禮拜天		lǐbàitiān	TW	Sunday 13
禮拜幾		lǐbàijǐ	TW	what day of the week? 13
豬		zhū	N	pig 9
豬肉		zhūròu	N	pork 11
每		měi-	SP	each, every 13

別	bié AV	(you) do not...! 10
夠	gòu SV	sufficient, enough 6
夠了。	gòu le. IE	(That's) enough 6
	--- A	sufficiently, enough 6
同	tóng- BF	sharing the same 11
同學	tóngxué N	fellow student 8; (term of address for someone in the same school as the speaker) 5
同事	tóngshì N	colleague 11
同姓	tóngxìng N	having the same surname 11
同名	tóngmíng N	having the same given name 11
同車	tóngchē N	being in the same vehicle 11
同船	tóngchuán N	being on the same ship 11
同（飛）機	tóng(fēi)jī N	being in the same airplane 11
同屋	tóngwū	roommate 11
定	dìng	(decide, fix)
一定	yídìng A	definitely, certainly
一定要	yídìng yào	must, have to 9
興	xìng	(happy)
高興	gāoxìng SV	happy 11
	*xīng	(rise)
中興	Zhōngxīng BF	Revival (in names of institutions and business establishments)
中興樓	Zhōngxīng Lóu PW	Revival House (restaurant)

再	zài A	again, then (in the future) 7
影	yǐng	(shadow)
電影（兒）	diànyǐng,	movie, film 13
	diànyěngr N	
過	-guò, -guo VS	(completed action) 12
你吃過飯了嗎？	nǐ chīguo fàn le ma?	Have you eaten?
	-guo VS	(at least one occurrence of the action of the verb) 12
你吃過中國飯嗎？	nǐ chīguo Zhōngguo fàn ma?	Have you ever eaten Chinese food?
回	huí	(return)
回來	huí lai V	come back 11
回去	huí qu V	go back 11
回家	*huí jiā VO	come/go (back) home 15
玩（兒）	wán, wár V	play, have fun, have a good time, play with 13
因	yīn	(because of)
因爲	yīnwei CA	because 13

New uses for old characters

塊	-kuài M	piece 7
前天	qiántian TW	day before yesterday 13
大前天	dàqiántian TW	three days ago 13
後天	hòutian TW	day after tomorrow 13

那（一）天	nèi(yi)tiān TW	that day (in the past) 11
有一天	yǒu yìtiān CA	one day 10
那麼	nèmma CA	in that case 13
要是	yàoshi MA	if 13
就	jiù A	as a consequence, then 13
快	kuài A	close to, nearly 13
生	shēng V	be born 13
來	lái V	(come and) be here 13
走	zǒu V	(depart and) be away 13
晚	wǎn *SV	late 18
不要	búyào AV	(you) do not...! 10

III. Phrases and sentences

年
前年。去年。明年。今年。後年。大後年。大前年。年年。

月
上個月。下個月。這個月。那個月。去年三月。明年五月。

時
甚麼時候了?時候不早了。時候太晚了。

候
沒去。昨天誰來了?昨天他母親來了。

昨
昨天晚上。昨天早上。昨天他

禮
禮拜幾?禮拜天。昨天是禮拜幾?昨天是禮拜六。上禮拜你朋友沒來嗎?他上禮拜來。

拜
不能來。他說他這個禮拜來。

豬
豬肉。幾分錢的豬肉。他吃豬肉不吃?他不吃豬肉。豬肉貴,牛肉貴?豬肉貴。

每
每一個月。每年一月。每人一條魚。每人一塊肉。每人五塊錢。每天他都不吃早飯。他每天晚上都喝一點兒酒。

別
別吃了。別買了。別說了。別看了。別打了。

夠
夠不夠?甚麼夠不夠?錢夠不夠?不夠。夠大嗎?夠大。

同　同學。張同學。同船。同事。同
　　姓。同名。同車。同機。同屋。

玩　到甚麼地方去玩？到英
　　國去玩。那個孩子玩
　　甚麼？他玩小船。

定　一定。一定來。一定去。一定不
　　飛機去。明天一定不坐飛機去。

再　再買一個。再吃一點兒。再想
　　一想。再看一看。再問一問。

興　高興。真高興。我們都很高興。
　　中興。中興書店。

影　電影。外國電影。中國電影。
　　法國電影。

因　因為。因為天氣不好，
　　他沒來。因為他的
　　朋友都不在這裏。

過　去過。沒去過。看過。沒看過。
　　看過沒看過？

回　回來。回去。她今天一定要回去。
　　她從紐約回去。回家。

IV. Sentences (regular characters)

1. 昨天來看你的那個人，他姓甚麼？—他姓毛。

2. 北京樓的菜真好。他們做的菜，每一個菜我都喜歡吃。

3. 我每個禮拜都看電影；有的時候一個晚上看兩個電影。

4. 要是菜不夠，請你告訴我，我可以再要一個。

5. 這幾天因爲我父母來看我，我沒怎麼念書。

6. 那個飯舘叫中興樓，不叫北京樓。

7. 今天下那麼大的雨，可是你們都來了，我真高興。

8. 國新要說話的時候，他母親說：「別說話！你開車的時候，別說話！」

9. 要是禮拜天是每一個禮拜的第一天，那麼怎麼能說是禮拜一？ Monday

10. 他是一九五六年生的，我也是那年生的。我們是同年。

11. 他今年回過家了嗎？

V. Longer passage

上禮拜五我請了六個朋友在家裏吃飯。這六個朋友，有三個是我的同學。

禮拜三晚上，姓高的同學打電話來，說：「你請我吃飯，有些甚麼好菜？」我說：「你來不來？」他說：「你告訴我有些甚麼好菜我就來。」

我再問他：「你來不來？」他說：「我一定來。」

禮拜四早上姓錢的那個同學打電話來，說：「你明天晚上請我吃飯，是不是吃魚？要是吃魚，我不來。」我說：你來吧，

我們明天有好幾個菜；有魚也有肉。」

禮拜五晚上快吃飯的時候，姓張的同學打電話來，說：「你是不是今天晚上請我吃飯？」我說：「是，你快來吧。」

我那三個同學都來了，我那三個朋友也都來了。我說：「高同學，我知道你喜歡吃牛肉，我買了不少牛肉，請你做牛肉吧！

張同學，上個月你請我們吃飯，你做的那些中國菜，我們都

說好吃，請你做兩個中國菜吧！錢同學，我知道你喜歡吃豬肉，你做豬肉吧！」他們三個人都不說話。我跟他們說：「我這三個朋友都住在紐約。他們都知道你們三個人很會做菜；大前天一請他們，他們就都說他們一定要來吃你們三個人做的菜。」我這三個同學都看了看我，就都去做飯去了。

那天晚上，因為我這三個同學做的菜很好吃，我這三個朋友很高興，我這三個同學也很高興，我們都很高興。

VI. Sentences (simplified characters)

1. 昨天来看你的那个人，他姓什么？一他姓毛。

2. 北京楼的菜真好。他们做的菜，每一个菜我都喜欢吃。

3. 我每个礼拜都看电影；有的时候一个晚上看两个电影。

4. 要是菜不够，请你告诉我，我可以再要一个。

5. 这几天因为我父母来看我，我没怎么念书。

6. 那个饭馆叫中兴楼，不叫北京楼。

7. 今天下那么大雨，可是你们都来了，我真高兴。

8. 国新要说话的时候，他母亲说：「别说话！你开
   车的时候，别说话！」

9. 要是礼拜天是每一个礼拜的第一天，那么怎么能说
   Monday 是礼拜一？

10. 他是一九五六年生的，我也是那年生的。我们是同年。

11. 他今年回过家了吗？

Lesson 12

(After SSC 14)

I. <u>Preparation</u>

12.1 <u>"Before" and "after"</u> (S 14.N4). The time words <u>yǐqián</u> "time before"
and <u>yǐhòu</u> "time after" occur in topic position, either alone or preceded by a
modifying expression. Alone, <u>yǐqián</u> means "previously" and <u>yǐhòu</u> means "afterward, from now on". Preceded by a modifying expression, <u>X yǐqián</u> means "before
X" and <u>X yǐhòu</u> means "after X".

以前我在中國	yǐqián, wǒ zài Zhōngguo.	Previously, I was in China.
一九七五以前，我在中國。	yī-jiǔ-qī-wǔ yǐqián, wǒ zài Zhōngguo.	I was in China before 1975.
以後我在日本教書。	yǐhòu, wǒ zài Rìběn jiāo shū.	Afterwards, I taught in Japan.
我吃晚飯以後，寫了一封信。	wǒ chī wǎnfàn yǐhòu, xiěle yìfēng xìn.	I wrote a letter after I had eaten supper.

In the last example, notice the absence of <u>le</u> in the modifying clause.
    Another way of expressing "after" is to use the verb <u>guò</u> "pass" with an
expression denoting an amount of time as its object. This <u>guò X</u> expression
may then occur in topic position, meaning "at the passing of X amount of time",
or more simply "after X". In past-tense sentences, <u>le</u> is optional after <u>guò</u>.

過（了）兩個禮拜她走了。	guò(le) liǎngge lǐbài, tā zǒu le.	She left after two weeks.

12.2 <u>Restrictions on the position of</u> yīnwei <u>"because"</u>(S 14.N5). In the

pattern yīnwei X, suóyi Y "Y, because X", if the subjects of both clauses are
identical, yīnwei may precede or follow any topic in its clause; in such
cases, yīnwei is a movable adverb. But in the same pattern, if the subjects
of the two clauses are different, yīnwei must precede any topic in its clause,
and hence is a conjunctive adverb. It is also a conjunctive adverb in the
pattern (X,) yīnwei Y, as for example in answer to a question.

她爲甚麼没來？　ta wèishemma méi-   Why didn't she come? -- Because
　—因爲她　　　　lái? -- yīnwei   she had no free time.
　没有工夫。　　　ta méiyou gōngfu.

她没來，因爲她　tā méilái, yīnwei   She didn't come, because she
　没有工夫。　　　ta méiyou gōngfu.   had no free time.

因爲她／她因爲　yīnwei ta / ta yīn-
　没有工夫，所　　wei méiyou gōngfu,
　以没來。　　　　suóyi méilái.

因爲她知道，我　yīnwei ta zhīdao,   I asked her, because she knows
　所以問了她了。　wǒ suóyi wènle   (about it).
　　　　　　　　　ta le.

    12.3 Question words as indefinites (S 14.1). Every Chinese question word
may also function as an indefinite. For example shémma "what?" functioning as
an indefinite may mean "any, anything, nothing". Indefinites occur in questions with ma (S 14.1.1), in negative sentences (S 14.1.2), and as topics of
positve sentences with dōu or negative sentences with dōu or yě (S 14.1.3).

你要甚麼嗎？　nǐ yào shémma ma?   Do you want anything?

我不要甚麼。　wǒ búyào shémma.   I don't want anything.

我甚麼也不要。wǒ shémma yě búyào. I don't want anything (at all).

我甚麼都要。　wǒ shémma dōu yào.   I want everything.

    In negative sentences, replacing the indefinite topic with yì-M (N) intensifies the negative universal meaning (S 14.2).

我一分錢，   wǒ yīfēn qián,   I don't want a cent.

也不要。   yě búyào.

    12.4 <u>Restrictions on the bound form</u> -jíle "extremely" (S 11.N9). The intensifying suffix <u>-jíle</u> is added to stative verbs that are normally not negated. It is added to compound stative verbs of the type <u>hǎo-V</u> / <u>nán-V</u> (6.2) but not normally to compound stative verbs of the type <u>yǒu-N</u> (6.1). The expression <u>SV-jíle</u> is limited to comment position.

那個孩子聰明   nèige háizi,   That child is extremely bright.

極了。   cōngmingjíle.

那個孩子好看   nèige háizi,   That child is extremely good-

極了。   hǎokànjíle.   looking.

New characters

筷	客	半	久
13　118.7　竹	9　40.6　宀	5　24.3　十	3　4.2　丿
對	封	用	工
14　41.11　寸	9　41.6　寸	5　101.0　用	3　48.0　工
算	得	共	公
14　118.8　竹	11　60.8　彳	6　12.4　八	4　12.2　八
聰	情	忙	夫
17　128.11　耳	11　61.8　心	6　61.3　心	4　37.1　大
覺	極	信	日
20　147.13　見	13　75.9　木	9　9.7　人	4　72.0　日

Variant form

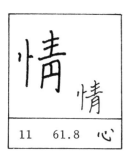

情

| 11 | 61.8 | 心 |

Simplified forms

极 极 極	对 对 對	聪 聪 聰	觉 觉 覺
8 75.4 木	5 41.2 寸	15 128.9 耳	9 147.5 見

II. New words

工		gōng	(work)
夫		fū	(man)
	工夫	gōngfu N	free time; time 13
共		gòng	(collectively)
	一共	yígòng A	altogether, in all 6
公		gōng	(public)
	公里	-gōnglǐ M	kilometer 6
	公共	gōnggòng BF	public
	公共汽車	gōnggòngqìchē N	(public) bus 11
	公共汽車站	gōnggòngqìchē-zhàn N	bus stop; bus station 11
信		xìn N (M: -fēng)	letter 14
	寫信	xiě xìn VO	write (letters) 14
封		-fēng M	(to seal:) (letters) 14
	信封（兒）	*xìnfēng(r) N	envelope
忙		máng SV	busy 2
		--- *V	busy about 16; *be in a rush
對		duì SV	correct, right 11
	對了。	duì le. IE	That's right. 8
	不對。	búduì. IE	Wrong. 8
覺		jué	(wake up)
得		dé	(get)
	覺得	juéde V	feel that, be of the opinion that 11
		děi AV	must, have to, ought to 8

客	kè	(guest)
客氣	kèqi SV	polite, standing on ceremony 14
別客氣（了）	bié kèqi (le). IE	Don't stand on ceremony. 14
客人	*kèren N	guest 22; *customer
用	yòng V	use 14
不用	búyòng AV	need not 14
	--- CV	using, with 14
筷	kuài	(chopsticks)
筷子	kuàizi N	chopsticks 14
久	jiǔ SV	long (time) 13
聰	cōng	(clear of hearing)
聰明	cōngming SV	intelligent, bright
極	jí	(extreme)
極了	-jíle BF	extremely 11
半	bàn NU	half 6
半本書	bànběn shū	half a book
一本半書	yìběnbàn shū	a book and a half
一半（兒）	yíbàn, yíbàr N	half 6
算	suàn	(calculate)
打算	dǎsuan AV	plan to 11
情	qíng	(condition)
事情	shìqing N	job 7; matter, affair 14
日	-rì *M	day (of the month) (literary)
一日	yīrì TW	the first (day of the month)

三月二日   sānyuè èrrì TW   March 2nd

生日   shēngrì N   birthday 13

日本   Rìběn PW   Japan 5

New uses for old characters

汽水（兒）   qìshuǐ, qìshuěr N   carbonated soft drink, soda pop 12

別的   biéde N   other, remaining 14

別人   biéren N   other people, remaining people 14

上一站   shàngyízhàn PW   the last stop (before now) 14

下一站   xiàyízhàn PW   the next stop 14

本來   běnlái TW   original time, originally 11

以前   yǐqián TW   previously, before 14

以後   yǐhòu TW   afterward, after, from now on 14

所以   suóyi MA   therefore 14

新   xīn A   newly, recently 14

（還）是   (hái)shi CA   is (either)?, or is? 14

叫   jiào V   tell, ask (someone to do something)
                                           14

開   kāi V   open, begin operations 14

過   guò V   pass, go by, after 14

給   gěi CV   for, to 14

　給父母寫信   gěi fùmǔ   write to one's parents / write a
                 xiě xìn   letter for one's parents

寫給   *xiégei V   write to

　寫信給父母   xiě xìn   write to one's parents
                 gei fùmǔ

上來	shàng lai V	come up 14
上去	shàng qu V	go up 14
下來	xià lai V	come down 14
下去	xià qu V	go down 14
上車	shàng chē VO	get on a bus/train/trolley, get into a car 14
下車	xià chē VO	get off a bus/train/trolley, get out of a car 14
上船	shàng chuán VO	get onto a ship 14
下船	xià chuán VO	get onto a ship 14
上學	shàng xué VO	go to school 14
下學	xià xué VO	get out of school 14
好説。	hǎo shuō. IE	You flatter me. 14

III.　Phrases and sentences

工
工夫。有工夫。没工夫。三天

夫
的工夫。一點兒工夫也沒有。

共
一共。一共要多少塊錢?一共要八千四。一共有幾個人?一共，四個人。

公
公共汽車。公共汽車裏有好幾個人。公共汽車站。

信
寫信。寫信給誰?寫信給男朋友。

封
信封。一封信。兩封信。

忙
忙不忙?真忙。他忙甚麼?他不忙甚麼。

對
對不對?一點兒都不對。真對不對?一點兒都不對。是一點兒都不對。

覺
得
覺得。覺得很高興。覺得很高興。我們都覺得很高興。得去。得去念書。得看。得看三本書。

客
客氣。為甚麼他那麼客氣?別客氣了。客人。她是我的客人。我請了十幾個客人。客人都來了。客人都走了。

用
用筆。用筆寫字。用筆寫字。用中國筆寫字。用美國筆寫中國字不難。用毛筆寫英文字很難。

筷
筷子。用筷子。我不會用筷子。中國人用筷子吃飯。

久　多麼久?住了多久?學了多久?

聰　聰明。很聰明。那個孩子很聰明。

極　好極了。快極了。慢極了。好喝極了。

半　半個。半張。一張半。半塊錢的牛肉。一半。一半真聰明，一半不怎麼聰明。

算　打算。我打算明年到法國去。她打算下禮拜六到紐約去玩兒。

情　事情。做的事情。他做的事情。這是他做的事情。

日　日本。生日。一九七七年四月八日。

IV. Sentences (regular characters)

1. 他昨天請他的女朋友吃飯，他女朋友說，「沒有工夫。」今天他再請她，她還說，「沒有工夫。」

2. 那個學校在這個山後頭。學校前頭有一條路。你一過了這個山就是那條路。

3. 別忙，車還沒來呢。車來的時候我告訴你。

4. 你寫的那封信那麼長，是寫給你母親的嗎？

5. 你先走吧，過一會兒我可以坐公共汽車回家。

6. 我想了想他說的話不對。這條路沒有那麼長。他說的一定是公里，不是英里。

7. 她是今天早上去的。她說她得到紐約去買點兒東西。

8. 別人都會用筷子吃飯，就是我不會，我一定要學。

9. 他是你的客人，你怎麼那麼不客氣呢？

10. 那個學校，每一個學生都很聰明。

18　他要來多久？──他說，他不要來多久，就打算來幾天。

17　他說中文不難學。你覺得他說的話對不對？

16　他這幾天忙極了。

15　那本書上說他的生日是一七五九年八月四日。

14　上禮拜六我們幾個朋友在一塊兒喝酒吃飯，高興極了。

13　他以前做過甚麼事情，我真是一點兒都不知道。

12　我打算明年到紐約去看看。

11　那個孩子說要半張紙，那個賣紙的人沒賣給他。

V. <u>Sentences</u> (simplified characters)

1. 他昨天请他的女朋友吃饭，他女朋友说，「没有工夫。」
   今天他再请她，她还说，「没有工夫。」

2. 那个学校在这个山后头。学校前头有一条路。你一过了
   这个山就 是那条路。

3. 你先走吧，过一会儿我可以坐公共汽车回家。

4. 你写的那封信那么长，是写给你母亲的吗？

5. 别忙，车还没来呢。车来的时候我告诉你。

6. 我想了想他说的话不对。这条路没有那么长，他说的
   一定是公里，不是英里。

7. 她是今天早上去的。她说她得到纽约去买点东西。

8. 别人都会用筷子吃饭，就是我不会，我一定要学。

9. 他是你的客人，你怎么那么不客气呢？

10. 那个学校，每一个学生都 很聪明。

11. 那个孩子说要买半张纸，那个卖纸的没卖给他。

12. 我打算明年到纽约去看看。

13. 他以前做过什么事情，我真是一点儿都 不知道。

14. 上礼拜六我们几个朋友在一块儿喝酒吃饭，高兴
    极了。

15. 那本书上说他的生日是一七五九年八月四日。

16. 他这几天忙极了。今天早上他跟我说他不能到纽
约去。

17. 他说中文不难学。你觉得他说的话对不对？

18. 他要来多久？—他说，他不要来多久，就打算来几天。

Lesson 13

(After SSC 15)

I. Preparation

13.1 <u>Stative verbs denoting manner.</u> In addition to their function as stative verbs, <u>kuài, màn, duō,</u> and <u>shǎo</u> function as fixed adverbs in imperative sentences, where they denote the manner in which the action of the verb should be done (S 15.N3, S 15.1). <u>kuài, màn,</u> and certain other stative verbs also occur after functive verbs in imperative sentences in this pattern: <u>V (de) SV yìdiǎr</u> "Do the action of the verb more SV!" The corresponding negative imperative is: <u>bié V de nèmma SV</u> "Don't do the action of the verb in such a SV manner!" (S 15.2.1). The expression following the <u>de</u> is called a "manner comment". Indicative sentences with manner comments follow these patterns: <u>(S) V de (A) SV</u> "(S) did the action of the verb in a (A) SV manner", if the verb is intransitive, or if the verb is transitive but the object is unexpressed; <u>S V O, V de (A) SV</u> "S did the action of the verb on O in a (A) SV manner", if an object is expressed in an unmeasured form; and <u>(SP-NU-M) O, SV de (A) SV</u> (same meaning), an optional variant if the object is unmeasured, obligatory if the object is measured (S 15.2.2). The <u>de</u> preceding manner comments is now usually written 得 ; older texts use 的 .

快告訴我。	kuài gàosu wǒ.	Hurry up and tell me!
快一點兒說。	kuài yidiar shuō.	Hurry up and speak! / Speak faster!
說（得）快一點兒。	shuō (de) kuài yidiar.	Speak faster! / (Someone) spoke faster.
別說得那麼快。	bié shuō de nèmma kuài.	Don't speak so fast!
他說得很快。	ta shuō de hěn kuài.	He speaks very quickly.
他說話說得很快。	ta shuō huà, shuō de hěn kuài.	

他説中國話   ta shuō Zhōngguo   He speaks Chinese very well.
説得很好。   huà, shuō de
              hěn hǎo.

中國話，他説   Zhōngguo huà, ta
得很好。   shuō de hěn hǎo.

那句中國話，他   nèijù Zhōngguo   He said that sentence in Chinese
説得很好。   huà, ta shuō de   very well.
              hěn hǎo.

    13.2 <u>Grammar changes in long expressions</u>. In Chinese, length of ex-
pression affects grammatical usage. For example, there is a tendency to omit
<u>de</u> after a pronoun if it is the first in a series of two or more modifiers
(S 15.3). Again, in long non-content questions about past action, <u>'yǒu méiyǒ</u>
may precede the verb; the answer in such a case would be <u>yǒu</u> or <u>méiyou</u> (S 15.

我們學校的一個   wǒmen xuéxiào de   the older brother of a student
學生的哥哥   yige xuésheng   at our school
             de gēge

你有没有到城   ni 'yǒu meiyǒu   Have you ever eaten at that
外頭新開的   dao chéng wài-   new(ly opened) restaurant
那家飯舘兒   tou, xīn kāi de   outside the city? -- Yes,
去吃過飯？   neijia fànguǎr   I have.
—有。   qu chīguo fàn?
             -- yǒu.

New characters

廠	拿	作	史
15 53.12 广	10 64.6 手	7 9.5 人	5 30.2 口
廣	海	忘	句
15 53.12 广	10 85.1 水	7 61.4 心	5 30.2 口
趣	寄	於	民
15 156.8 走	11 40.8 宀	8 70.4 方	5 83.1 氏
歷	習	社	州
16 27.12 厂	11 124.5 羽	8 113.3 示	6 47.3 川
關	港	香	收
19 169.11 門	12 85.9 水	9 186.0 香	6 66.2 攴

Variant forms

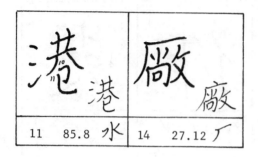

港 港	厰 厰
11 85.8 水	14 27.12 厂

Simplified forms

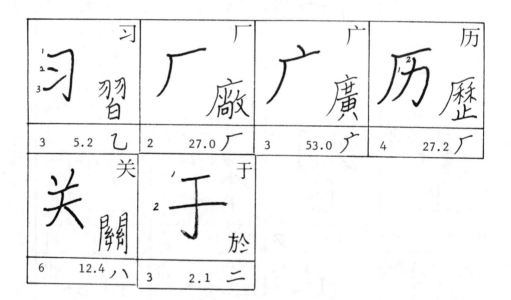

习 习 習	厂 厂 厰	广 广 廣	历 历 歷
3 5.2 乙	2 27.0 厂	3 53.0 广	4 27.2 厂
关 关 關	于 于 於		
6 12.4 八	3 2.1 二		

II. New words

廠	chǎng	(factory)
工廠	gōngchǎng N (M:)	factory 15)
	-jiā, -jiār)	
作	zuò	(compose)
工作	gōngzuò N	job 15
	--- V	work 15
社	shè	(organization)
公社	gōngshè N	commune 15
民	mín	(people)
人民	rénmín N	the people (of a country) 15
人民公社	rénmíngōngshè N	people's commune 15
收	shōu V	receive 15
收到	shōudào, shōudao V	receive 15
寄	jì V	mail 15
寄給	jǐgei V	mail to (someone) 15
寄到	jìdào V	get to (by mail) 15
習	xí	(practice)
學習	*xuéxí V	study 16
句	-jù M	(sentences) 15
三句話	sānjù huà	three sentences
句子	jùzi N	sentence 15
三個句子	sānge jùzi	three sentences
拿	ná V	grasp, take in the hand; manipulate; take, bring 14

	--- CV	taking in the hand, with 14
歷	lì	(pass through)
史	shǐ	(history)
歷史	lìshǐ N	history 15
趣	qù	(interest)
興趣	xìngqu N	interest 15
有興趣	yǒu xìngqu SV	interesting 15
	--- AV	be interested in 15
關	guān	(related)
於	yú	(to)
關於	guānyu CV	concerning, about 15
忘	wàng	(forget)
忘了	wàng le V	forget 15
海	hǎi	(sea)
上海	Shànghǎi PW	Shanghai 10
廣	guǎng	(broad)
州	zhōu	(province)
廣州	Guǎngzhōu PW	Canton 10
香	xiāng	(fragrant)
港	gǎng	(harbor)
香港	Xiānggǎng PW	Hong Kong 10
新港	Xīngǎng PW	New Haven 10

<u>New uses for old characters</u>

小説（兒）	xiǎoshuō(r) N	fiction; work of fiction;
	(M: -běn)	novel 15
工人	gōngren N	laborer, worker 15
工錢	*gōngqián N	wage, pay
萬里長城	*Wànlǐcháng- chéng PW	(ten-thousand <u>li</u> long wall:) the Great Wall
少	shǎo A	less 15
很少	hěn shǎo A	(very) seldom 15
有（一）點（兒）	yǒu yìdiǎr, yóu diar A	a bit 12
多	duō A	more 15
前	qián- SP	past 15
對	duì CV	(facing:) with respect to, to, in
來	lái V	come to 15
去	qù V	go to 15
回	huí *V	return to
飛	fēi *V	fly to
看到	kàndào V	read to; see as far as 15
念到	niàndào V	read to / as far as 15
學到	xuédào V	study as far as 15
寫到	xiědào V	write as far as 15
説到	shuōdào V	get to (in talking) 15
説	shuō V	talk about 10
想到	xiǎngdào V	(think as far as:) think, imagine 15

喝到	hēdào V	drink as far as 15
到	-dào, -dao VS	so that the actor successfully achieves the action of the verb 15
收到	shōudào, shōudao	receive 15
回信	huí xìn VO	send a letter in reply 15
慢走	màn zǒu. IE	(Leave slowly:) Goodbye. (Said to a parting guest.)
得／的	de P	(between a verb and a manner comment) 15

III. Phrases and sentences

廠 工廠。工廠很大。有很多家工廠。
汽車工廠。

作 工作。他在甚麼地方工作？他
工作的地方在哪條街？

社 公社。公社裏的人。公社裏的房子。

民 人民。人民公社。人民書店。

收 收到了女朋友的一封信。
收到了沒有？收到了甚麼了？

寄 寄信。寄給誰？寄給我父親。
寄到甚麼地方去？寄到英國去。

習 學習。學習寫字。學習畫。
畫兒。學習用打字機打字。

句 她就說了一句話。她說
的那句話是中文是英
文？她說的那句話是
中文。

拿 拿來。拿去。拿毛筆寫
字。拿筷子吃飯。

歷史 歷史。中國歷史。法國
歷史。英國歷史。

趣 興趣。有興趣。對畫畫
兒有興趣。

於關 關於念書的事。關於工
作的事。關於工廠的
事。關於公社的事。

忘 忘了。忘了甚麼了?忘了寫字了。

海 上海。上海飯店。到上海飯店去吃飯去。

廣 廣州。到廣州去。到廣州去學習做菜。

香港 香港。新港。新港的中國飯舘多不多?香港的中國飯舘兒呢?

IV. Sentences (regular characters)

1. 美國飛機工人的工錢很高。英國飛機工人的工錢是不是也那麼高？

2. 這一家汽車工廠，有三千工人；有男工人，也有女工人。

3. 這個人民公社很大，裏頭有兩個小工廠；每個工廠有五十多人在那裏工作。

4. 人民書店在那條街上，不在這條街上；你忘了嗎？

5. 寫字得學習，用筷子也得學習。

6. 那家飯舘做牛肉做得很好。可是他們做豬肉做得好不好，我不知道，因為我沒吃過。

7. 這個句子那麼長，那麼難說，一句就夠了。

8. 他去年在北京的時候，有沒有到萬里長城去過？

9. 錢先生是十二月回的英國。明年一月回來上課。

10. 先生叫我們每人做十五個句子。我們說，「每人做十句，

14　13　12　11

不是夠了嗎？」先生說，「好吧，那麼你們每人做十句吧！」

她拿來的那本書，不是我要的那一本法國歷史。

我對畫畫兒很有興趣，很想學，可是就是沒有工夫。

關於他要在廣州念書的事，我寫了信告訴我在廣州的朋友了。

要是你對這個工作有興趣，那麼你一定很喜歡去做，一點兒都不覺得難。

V. Longer passage

我的同屋昨天收到一封信，是從北京寄來的。寫信的這個人是他以前在紐約念書的時候的一個朋友。我的同屋說，「他這封信是用中文寫的，你可以看看。」

這封信說：「我上個月到的香港，在香港住了兩天，從香港坐火車到廣州，在廣州住了三天。從廣州我們坐飛機飛到上海，在上海我看了好幾個大工廠。上海真大，有很多地方我們都沒去過。

「我跟我幾個朋友現在都住在北京的一個學校裏。我們明天就到城外頭的一個人民公社去學習。北京城裏有不少很好看的地方，我們都看過了。昨天有一個朋友告訴我：下禮拜我們去看萬里長城，我高興極了。

「我們下個月從北京先飛到法國住兩天，再從法國飛美國。我們回紐約以後，一定到新港來看你。你叫我給你買的書，我都買了。要是你要我寄給你，請你寫信告訴我。」

　我看了這封信以後，我跟我的同屋説：「你這個同學的信寫得很好。他的中文是在哪兒學的？」我的同屋説：「他在好幾個學校學過。他學了快三年了。」

VI. Sentences (simplified characters)

1. 美国飞机工人的工钱很高。英国飞机工人的工钱是不是
   也那么高?

2. 这一家汽车工厂，有三千多工人。有男工人，也有女工人。

3. 这个人民公社很大，里头有两个小工厂。每个工厂有五十
   多人 在那里工作。

4. 人民书店在那条街上，不在这条街上；你忘了吗?

5. 写字得学习，用筷子也得学习。

6. 那家饭馆做牛肉做得很好。可是他们做猪肉 做得好
   不好，我不 知道，因为我没吃过。

7. 这个句子那么长，那么难说，一句就够了。

8. 他去年在北京的时候，有没有到万里长城 去过?

9. 钱先生是十二月回的英国。明年一月回来上课。

10. 先生叫我们每人做十五个句子。我们说，「每人做十句，
    不是 够了吗?」先生说，「好吧，那么你们每人做十句吧!」

11. 她拿来的那本书，不是我要的那一本法国历史。

12. 我对画画儿很有兴趣，很想学，可是就是没有工夫。

13. 关于他要在广州念书的事,我写了信告诉我在广州的朋友了。

14. 要是你对这个工作有兴趣，那么你一定很喜欢去做，一
    点儿都 不觉得难。

Lesson 14

(After SSC 16)

I.   Preparation

14.1   <u>Indefinite expressions of the type "two or three"</u> (S 6.8).   The
patterns are $\underline{NU_n\text{-}NU_{n+1}\text{-}M}$ and $\underline{NU_n\text{-}NU_{n+2}\text{-}M}$, with no Chinese equivalent of the
English "or".

兩三本	liǎng-sānběn	two or three volumes
三五個	sān-wǔge	three or (four, or four or) five

14.2   <u>The use of</u> líng <u>"zero, and"</u> (S 6.N14).   Some measures occur in
series of units, sub-units, sub-sub-units and so on.   Three such series have
been introduced so far: <u>-wànwàn, -qiānwàn, -bǎiwàn, -shíwàn, -wàn, -qiān,</u>
<u>-bǎi,</u> and <u>-shí</u> is one series; <u>-kuài, -máo,</u> and <u>-fēn</u> is another; <u>-nián, -ge yuè,</u>
and <u>-tiān</u> is the third.   When two or more members of a series of measures occur
in number expressions, the measure denoting the larger amount precedes one
denoting the smaller amount.   In such a number expression, if one or more adjacent internal NU-M phrases have "zero" for NU, <u>líng</u> replaces these phrases.
After <u>NU-nián, líng</u> precedes <u>NU-ge yuè</u>, as well as <u>NU-tiān</u>.

一萬零一百	yíwàn, líng yìbǎi	ten thousand and one hundred
一萬零一	yíwàn, líng yī	ten thousand and one
一塊零三分	yíkuài, líng sānfēn	one dollar and three cents
一年零三天	yìnián, líng sāntiān	one year and three days
一年零三個月	yìnián, líng sānge yuè	one year and three months

When numbers are said digit by digit, as in giving telephone numbers and
years, <u>líng</u> is said for every zero.

一零一零零	yī-líng-yī-líng- líng	one oh one oh oh
一零零零一	yī-líng-líng-líng- yī	one oh oh oh one
一九一零年	yī-jiǔ-yī-líng- nián	1910 (the year)

14.3 <u>The transposed actor (S 16.1)</u>. Placing the word denoting the actor after the verb has the effect of adding "comment" meaning to the word, emphasizing the fact that it is something new in the discourse and interesting to the speaker. Compare:

信來了。	xìn lái le.	The letter(s) arrived.
來信了。	lái xìn le.	A letter / Some letters arrived.

14.4 <u>More on the pivot (S 16.2)</u>. A pivot is always the object of the preceding verb and the topic of the following verb. Sometimes it is the recipient of the action of the preceding verb and the subject of the following one (S 6.12); sometimes it is the recipient of the action of the preceding verb and the transposed object of the following one; sometimes it is the transposed actor of the preceding verb and the topic of the following one.

有一個學生 　有錢。	yǒu yíge xuésheng, yǒu qián.	There is a student, (and he) has money. / There is a student who has money.
我們老師説了 　一個字學問 　我們没學過。	women lǎoshī shuōle yige zì xuéwen wǒmen méixuéguo.	Our teacher said a word that we haven't studied: <u>xuéwen</u>.

從外頭來了兩
　個客人坐在
屋子後頭。

cóng wàitou,
　láile liǎngge
kèren, zuòzai
wūzi hòutou.

Two guests came from
　outside and sat at the
back of the room.

New characters

臺 臺	研 研	星 星	江 江
14　133.8　至	11　112.6　石	9　72.5　日	6　85.3　水
層 層	敢 敢	參 參	希 希
15　44.12　尸	12　66.8　攴	11　28.9　厶	7　50.4　巾
聽 聽	期 期	商 商	究 究
22　128.16　耳	12　74.8　月	11　30.8　口	7　116.2　穴
灣 灣	華 華	啊 啊	和 和
25　85.22　水	12　140.8　艸	11　30.8　口	8　30.5　口
觀 觀	零 零	望 望	底 底
25　147.18　見	13　173.5　雨	11　74.7　月	8　53.5　广

Variant forms

呀 啊	零 零雨	台 臺	層 層尸
7 30.4 口	13 173.5 雨	5 30.2 口	15 44.12 尸

Simplified forms

参 参 参	研 研 研	华 华 華 十	台 台 臺
8 28.6 厶	9 112.6 石	6 24.4 十	5 30.2 口
层 层 層	听 听 聽	湾 湾 灣	观 观 觀
7 44.4 尸	7 30.4 口	12 85.9 水	6 147.2 見

14.5 <u>Another radical.</u>

No. 112 <u>shí</u> 石 "stone": 研 .

II.   New words

華	huá	(China)
中華	Zhōnghuá BF	China (in names of companies, organizations, etc.) 16
中華民國	Zhōnghuá Mínguó N	Republic of China 16
華山	Huá Shān N	Mt. Hua 5
和	hé	(harmony)
共和國	gònghéguó N	republic 16
中華人民 共和國	Zhōnghuá Rénmín Gònghéguó N	People's Republic of China 16
聽	tīng	(hear)
聽説	tīng shuō V	(I) hear (it said) that 10
啊，呀	a, ya *	(question particle) 9; (exclamatory particle) 12 (For the pronunciation, see S 9.N9.)
研	yán	(grind)
究	jiù	(source)
研究	yánjiu V	study, do research on 15
	--- N	study, research 15
有研究	yǒu yánjiu SV	well versed 16

---

*Some authors use one or the other of these two forms no matter what the pronunciation of the sentence particle. Others carefully distinguish the two main spoken forms of the particle when they write and use 呀 for ya and 啊 for all other forms.

希	xī	(hope)
望	wàng	(gaze)
希望	xīwàng V	hope, wish 15
	--- N	hope, wish 15
有希望	yǒu xīwàng SV	promising 15
臺	tái	(platform)
臺北	Táiběi PW	Taipei 10
灣	wān	(cove)
臺灣	Táiwān, Táiwan PW	Taiwan 12
臺灣大學	Táiwān Dàxué PW	(National) Taiwan University 12
臺大	Tái Dà	Taiwan U. 12
敢	gǎn AV	dare 15
我不敢說。	wǒ bùgǎn shuō.	(I don't dare say:) I don't know.
星	xīng	(star)
期	qī	(period)
星期	xīngqī N	week 13
星期一	xīngqīyī TW	Monday 13
星期二	xīngqīèr TW	Tuesday 13
星期日／天	xīngqīrì/-tiān TW	Sunday 13
參	cān	(take part in)
觀	guān	(observe)
參觀	cānguān V	visit (a place to examine its facilities) 15

商　　　　　　　shāng　　　　　　　　(merchandise)

　商店　　　　　shāngdiàn　　　　　　store 10

　　　　　　　　　(M: -jiā)

江　　　　　　　jiāng　　　　　　　　(river); Chiang 5

　長江　　　　　Cháng Jiāng N　　　　Yangtze River 5

零　　　　　　　líng NU　　　　　　　zero; and (in numbers) 6

底　　　　　　　dǐ　　　　　　　　　(bottom)

　底下　　　　　dǐxia PW　　　　　　area underneath 10

　　樓底下　　　lóu dǐxia PW　　　　downstairs 10

層　　　　　　　-céng M　　　　　　　layer, story, level 14

New uses for old characters

學問　　　　　　xuéwen N　　　　　　learning, knowledge 16

　有學問　　　　yǒu xuéwen SV　　　　learned 16

　研究學問　　　yánjiu xuéwen VO　　do research 16

本子，本兒　　　běnzi, běr N　　　　notebook 16

從前　　　　　　cóngqián TW　　　　the past; formerly 16

老　　　　　　　lǎo SV　　　　　　venerable, elderly, old 16

　老朋友　　　　lǎopéngyou N　　　　old friend 16

　　　　　　　　--- BF　　　　　　　(prefixed to surnames) 16

走　　　　　　　zǒu V　　　　　　　walk, go 16

　走到　　　　　zǒudao V　　　　　　walk to, go to 16

　　　　　　　　--- VS　　　　　　　so that the recipient of the actio

　　　　　　　　　　　　　　　　　　of the verb moves away from the

　　　　　　　　　　　　　　　　　　speaker; away 16

上	-shang VS	so that the action of the verb proceeds upwards; up (with <u>lai</u> and <u>qu</u>) 16
下	-xia VS	so that the action of the verb proceeds downwards; down (with <u>lai</u> and <u>qu</u>) 16
不	bù. IE	No. 16
機會	jīhui N	opportunity, chance 15

III. Phrases and sentences

華 中華飯店。中華民國。華山。

和 共和國。中華人民共和國。
美國是一個共和國。

聽 聽説。聽説明天下雨。聽説
他很愛喝酒。

啊 呀 他來不來呀?他弟弟來不來
呀?你們去不去啊?那好
啊。別給她呀!

研 究 研究。研究甚麼?喜歡研究
甚麼?喜歡研究歷史。

希 望 希望。有希望。有很大的希

望。希望你們能來。希望
你們都能來。希望你們
下禮拜都能來。

臺 臺北。臺北有好大學嗎?
臺北有兩三個好大學。

灣 臺灣。臺灣大學。臺灣大
學在臺北。

敢 敢説,也敢做。他這個人
敢説敢做。他來不來,我
不敢説。

星 期 星期。星期四。星期四下午。
下星期四下午,我有工夫。

參 參觀。參觀你們的大學。到
臺大去參觀參觀。

觀

商 商店。臺北的商店。紐約的
商店。那一家商店很好嗎？
那一家商店很好嗎？

江 長江。長江有多長？有三千四百
三十英里長。江小姐。江小姐
的妹妹。

零 一萬零一。一年零三天。九千七
百零五。

底 底下。樓底下。樓底下有人
嗎？樓底下沒有人。

層 那個樓很高，有五十六層。一

百零四層的樓。那個火
車站有兩層。

IV. <u>Longer passages (regular characters)</u>

（一）

A: 聽說有一個中國電影。你想去看看嗎？

B: 那個電影叫甚麼名字啊？

A: 叫「新長江」。

B: 誰去看過？

A: 高美真看過。

B: 她說好不好？

A: 她說很好。

B: 好，我們也去看看。

（二）

A: 那個學校的電話是不是五零零五五零零？

B: 不是。是五零五零零五五。

（三）

A: 這本書是不是她的？

B: 這一本不是。這一本底下的那一本是。

（四）

A: 你開這個車吧！

B: 這個車我不敢開。

A: 為甚麼？

B: 我就開過小車，沒開過大車。這個車太大，我不敢開。

（五）

A：我怎麼可以到中華人民共和國去？

B：你可以坐飛機飛到法國去。到了法國以後，從法國坐飛機到北京去。

（六）

A：你打算學甚麼？

B：我打算學歷史。

A：學哪國歷史？

B：美國歷史跟中國歷史。

A：你對中國歷史真有興趣嗎？

B：是。去年我有兩個同學到中國去。一個去臺灣，一個去北京。他們回來告訴我很多關於中國這個國家的事情。我覺得中國這個國家有這麼長的歷史，要是我有工夫研究研究，一定很有意思。

A：他們是甚麼時候去的？

B：都是六月去的。

A：他們在中國住了多久？

B：一個在臺北住了兩個半月。一個在北京住了三個月。

A：他們在中國的時候住在甚麼地方？

B：一個住在他老師的朋友的家

裏。一個住在人民公社裏。

他們參觀了很多地方。

A　他們想再去嗎？

B　他們都想再去。他們都說
以後再有機會，他們一定
再去。

A　你希望到中國去看看嗎？

B　我希望我明年能去。

（七）

紐約城裏有一家商店大極了，
有十幾層樓。這家商店賣的東
西都很好，也不太貴。所以在城外
頭住的人也都喜歡到那兒去買東

西。每個星期六都有很多人從
城外頭開車到那兒去買東西。

V. Longer passages (simplified characters)

（一）

A　听说有一个中国电影。你想去看看吗？

B　那个电影叫什么名字啊？

A　叫「新长江」。

B　谁去看过？

A　高美真看过。

B　她说好不好？

A　她说很好。

B　好，我们也去看看。

（二）

A　那个学校的电话是不是五零零五五零零？

B　不是。是五零五零零五五。

（三）

A　这本书是不是她的？

B　这一本不是。这一本底下的那一本是。

（四）

A　你开这个车吧！

B　这个车我不敢开。

A　为什么？

B　我就开过小车，没开过大车。这个车太大，我不敢开。

（五）

A 我怎么可以到中华人民共和国去？

B 你可以坐飞机飞到法国去。到了法国以后，从法国飞
到北京去。

（六）

A 你打算学什么？

B 我打算学历史。

A 学哪国历史？

B 美国历史跟中国历史。

A 你对中国历史真有兴趣吗？

B 是。去年我有两个同学到中国去。一个去台湾，一个去北京。
他们回来告诉我很多关于中国的事情。我觉得中国这
个国家有这么长的历史，要是我有工夫研究研究，
一定很有意思。

A 他们是什么时候去的？

B 都是六月去的。

A 他们在中国住了多久？

B 一个在台北住了两个半月，一个在北京住了三个月。

A 他们在中国的时候住在什么地方？

B 一个住在他老师的朋友的家里。一个住在人民公社
里。他们参观了很多地方。

A 他们想再去吗？

B 他们都想再去。他们都说以后再有机会，他们一定再去。

A　　你希望到中国去看看吗？

B　　我希望我明年能去。

（七）

纽约城里有一家商店大极了，有十几层楼。这家商店卖的东西都很好，也不太贵，所以在城外头住的人也都喜欢到那儿去买东西。每个星期六都有很多人从城外头开车到那儿去买东西。

Lesson 15 (After SSC 16)

I. Preparation

綠 綠	紅 紅	行 行	出 出
14　120.8 糸	9　120.3 糸	6　144.0 行	5　17.3 凵
幫 幫	着 着	助 助	它 它
17　50.14 巾	12　109.7 目	7　19.5 力	5　40.2 宀
謝 謝	黑 黑	找 找	平 平
17　149.10 言	12　203.0 黑	7　64.4 手	5　51.2 干
邊 邊	葉 葉	係 係	正 正
19　162.15 辵	13　140.9 艸	9　9.7 人	5　77.1 止
願 願	圖 圖	南 南	白 白
19　181.10 頁	14　31.11 囗	9　24.7 十	5　106.0 白

Variant forms

牠 它	糸 係	着 着	著 着
7 93.3 牛	7 120.1 糸	11 109.6 目	13 140.9 艹
圖 圖	綠 綠	幫 幚	幫 幫
14 31.11 口	15 120.9 糸	12 50.9 巾	10 50.7 巾

Simplified forms

系 係	红 紅	叶 葉	图 圖
7 120.1 糸	6 120.3 糸	5 30.2 口	8 31.5 口
绿 綠	帮 幫	谢 謝	边 邊
11 120.8 糸	10 50.7 巾	12 149.10 言	5 162.2 辵
愿 願			
14 16.10 心			

15.1 <u>Another radical.</u>

No. 19 力 lì "power": 助

II. <u>New words</u>

圖	tú	(chart)
地圖	dìtú N	map 16
圖書舘	túshūguǎn N	library 16
邊（兒）	biān, biār N	side 10
	--- M	side 10
一邊 X ，一邊 Y	*yìbiān X,	X and Y at the same time
	yìbiān Y IE	
一邊説話，一邊吃飯	yìbiān shuō huà yìbiān chī fàn	talk and eat at the same time
四邊	sìbiān PW	all four sides, everywhere 10
	-bian, -biar BF	(suffix in placewords) 12
上邊	shàngbian PW	surface, top, above 12
下邊	xiàbian PW	bottom, below 12
裏邊	lǐbian PW	inside 12
外邊	wàibian PW	outside 12
前邊	qiánbian PW	front 12
後邊	hòubian PW	back 12
着	-zhe VS	(used in affirmative commands; indicates that the action or state denoted by the verb is continuing) 16
聽着	tīngzhe.	Listen.

下着雨呢。　　　xiàzhe yǔ ne.　　　It's raining.

一邊説着話，　yìbiān shuōzhe huà,　talking and eating at the

　一邊吃飯。　　yìbiān chī fàn　　　same time

找　　　　　　　zhǎo V　　　　　look for; call on, visit 10

行。　　　　　　xíng. IE　　　　　(go:) It is acceptable / OK. 4

　行不行？—　　'xíng bùxíng?　　　Would it be all right? -- No,

　不行。　　　　-- bùxíng.　　　　it wouldn't.

幫　　　　　　　bāng V　　　　　help, assist 16

　幫着　　　　　bāngzhe V　　　　help, assist 16

　幫忙　　　　　bāng máng VO　　help, assist 16

助　　　　　　　zhù　　　　　　(help)

　幫助　　　　　bāngzhu V/N　　help, assist(ance) 16

　　有幫助　　　yǒu bāngzhu SV　helpful 16

平　　　　　　　píng　　　　　　(level)

　北平　　　　　Běipíng PW　　　Peiping 10

　小平　　　　　Xiǎopíng N　　　Hsiao-p'ing (a given name) 8

　和平　　　　　hépíng N　　　　peace 15

　公平　　　　　*gōngpíng SV　　fair, equitable

謝　　　　　　　xiè　　　　　　(thank)

　謝謝　　　　　xièxie. IE　　　Thanks. 2

願　　　　　　　yuàn　　　　　(desire)

　願意　　　　　yuànyi AV　　　want to 7

出　　　　　　　chū　　　　　　(emerge)

　出來　　　　　chū lai V　　　come out 12

　出去　　　　　chū qu V　　　go out 12

		--- VS	so that the action emerges from
			a place; out (with <u>lai</u> and <u>qu</u>) 16
飛出來／去	fēichu lai/qu V	fly out 16
走出來／去	zǒuchu lai/qu V	walk out 16
開出來／去	kāichu lai/qu V	drive out 16
它	tā N	it (16.3)
南	nán L	south 16
南邊	nánbian PW	south 16
南京	Nánjīng PW	Nanking 10
紅	hóng	(red)
紅的	hóngde N	something red; red 9
紅茶	*hóngchá N	black tea
小紅書	*Xiǎo Hóngshū N	Little Red Book (of quotations
		from Mao Tse-tung)
綠	lǜ	(green)
綠的	lǜde N	something green; green 9
黑	hēi	(black)
黑的	hēide N	something black; black 9
白	bái	(white)
白的	báide N	something white; white 9
明白	míngbai V	understand clearly 16
白天	báitian TW	daytime, during the day 16
白菜	*báicài N	Chinese cabbage, celery cabbage
正	zhèng A	just (now) exactly, be right in
		the process of ...-ing 10

正在	zhèngzai A	(same meaning) 10
正好	zhèng hǎo. IE	Just right. 6
正是	zhèngshi A	just (during), exactly (during) 13
係	xì	(bind)
關係	guānxi N	connection, relevance 16
没有關係	méiyou guānxi. IE	Never mind. 7
葉	yè	(leaf)
葉子	yèzi N	leaf (of a tree, etc.) 13
紅葉	hóngyè N	red leaves, colored leaves (of autumn) 13

New uses for old characters

小方	Xiǎofāng N	Hsiao-fang (a given name) 14
東	dōng L	east 16
東邊	dōngbian PW	east 16
東南	dōngnán PW	southeast 16
西	xī L	west 16
西邊	xībian PW	west 16
西南	xīnán PW	southwest 16
北	běi L	north 16
北邊	běibian PW	north 16
東北	dōngběi PW	northeast; Manchuria 16
西北	xīběi PW	northwest 16
東南西北	dōng-nán-xī-běi	north, south, east, west 16
東西南北	dōng-xī-nán-běi	(same meaning)

III. Phrases and sentences

圖 地圖。中國地圖。圖書館。學校裏的圖書館。

邊 前邊。前邊的那個站。後邊。後邊的那所房子。四邊。
四邊都是水。

着 看着報呢。一邊看着報，一邊吃早飯。我們走着去吧。

找 找甚麼？找一條街。找一條街的名字。

行 行不行？不行。行了。

幫 幫誰？幫着誰？幫誰的忙？幫他的忙。幫他做甚麼？
幫他做飯。

助 幫助。很大的幫助。有很大的幫助。

平 北平。小平。小方跟小平。和平。公平。

謝 謝謝。謝謝你幫我的忙。

願 願意。願意做。願意做甚麼？願意教書。願意教英文。

出 出去。走出去。飛出去。飛出房子外頭去。

它　叫它甚麼？叫它甚麼名字？叫它小豬吧。

南　南京。南邊兒。東南。西南。

紅　紅的。紅的書。小紅書。紅茶。

綠　綠的。我很喜歡綠的那個。我看綠的跟紅的都好看。

白　白的。明白。白菜。白天。

黑　黑的。黑的筆。在黑的紙上寫白的字。

正　正看着報呢。正在看着報呢。正在看着今天早上的報呢。

係　關係。有關係。沒有關係。有很大的關係。

葉　葉子。紅葉。這個禮拜的紅葉。葉子有些是紅的有些是綠的。

IV.　Sentences (regular characters)

1　我汽車上有這個城的地圖。我去拿去。

2　他們的房子，前邊是路，後邊是山。

3　她喜歡一邊看着報，一邊吃早飯。

4　他說他要找一個東西，可是他没告訴我他要找甚麼。

5　我說，「你明天找，行不行？」他說不行，他要現在找。

6　我說，「我幫你找找吧。」他說，「你知道我找甚麼嗎？」

7　我要幫助他，可是他不告訴我他要找甚麼，我怎麼能幫助

8　我們說我們要和平，可是要是有很多的事情不公平，那麼怎麼能有和平呢？

9　謝謝你昨天給我的那本歷史書。我希望我每天都能看一點兒。

10　他說他願意研究中國歷史，因爲他對中國歷史有興趣。

11 從圖書館走出來的那個人是張國新的父親。

12 那個地方從前叫甚麼我不知道。現在都叫它北京。

13 她說南京北京她都住過好幾年。兩個地方都很好。

14 那本小紅書是上禮拜六我在紐約買的。

15 你明白那張畫的意思嗎？

16 為甚麼那張畫上的山有些地方是綠的，有些地方是紅的？

17 用這個筆寫字不太黑。

18 這個時候正是他上課的時候。

19 這個事情跟那個事情有很大的關係。

20 有些葉子是紅的，有些葉子還是綠的，真是好看極了。

V. Dialogs

(一)

A: 你到哪兒去？

B: 到圖書舘去。

A: 外邊兒下着雨呢。爲甚麼要到圖書舘去呢？

B: 我要找一個地圖。

A: 我有一個地圖，你看看行不行？

B: 行。

A: 你找甚麼地方，我給你找。

B: 你能幫着我找，好極了。

A: 這個城不大，叫長安(Cháng-ān)是不是這個？這個從前叫長安，現在不叫長安了。

B: 現在叫甚麼？

A: 現在叫西安(Xī'ān)了。你要找的是不是就是這個城？

B: 是，就是這個城。謝謝你。

(二)

A: 你怎麼來的？

B: 我走着來的。

A: 你沒開車來嗎？

B: 我覺得今天天氣這麼好，走走也很好。你願意出去走走嗎？

A: 走到哪兒去？

B 走到那個小山去，好不好？

B 那個小山有沒有中國名字？

A 我叫它東山。

B 是東西南北那個東嗎？

A 你說得很對。

B 前幾天紅葉正是好看的時候，我們到西山去看了看。真是美極了。這兒的紅葉每年都是那麼好看嗎？

A 不一定。我想這跟天氣有關係，要是下雨下得太多了，不行；下得太少了也不行。今年的雨，下得正好，所以這些紅葉真是美極了。

（三）

A 我下個月，打算請幾個老朋友吃晚飯。我不知道他們都有工夫沒有。

B 你請我不請？要是你請我，我甚麼時候都有工夫。

A 要是你幫着我做菜，我就請你。

B 我做的菜那麼不好吃，誰要吃我的菜呀？

A 你太客氣，你做的菜，誰都說好吃。

B 那麼你就請我吧，我一定來。

VI. <u>Sentences (simplified characters)</u>

1. 我汽车上有一个地图。我去拿去。

2. 他们的房子，前边是路，后边是山。

3. 她喜欢一边看着报，一边吃早饭。

4. 他说他要找一个东西，可是他没告诉我他要找什么。

5. 我说，「你明天找，行不行？」他说不行，他要现在找。

6. 我说，「我帮你找找吧。」他说，「你知道我找什么吗？」

7. 我要帮助他，可是他不告诉我他要找什么，我怎么能帮助
   他呢？

8. 我们说我们要和平，可是要是有很多的事情都不公平，

   那么怎么能有和平呢？

9. 谢谢你昨天给我的历史书。我希望我每天都能看一点儿。

10. 他说他愿意研究中国历史，因为他对中国历史有兴趣。

11. 从图书馆走出来的那个人是张国新的父亲。

12. 那个地方从前叫什么我不知道，现在都叫它北京。

13. 她说南京北京她都住过好几年。两个地方都很好。

14. 那本小红书是上礼拜六我在纽约买的。

15. 你明白那张画的意思吗？

16. 为什么那张画上的山有些地方是绿的，有些地方是红的？

17. 用这个笔写字不太黑。

18. 这个时候正是他上课的时候。

19. 这个事情跟那个事情有很大的关系。

20. 有些叶子是红的，有些叶子还是绿的，真是好看极了。

Index of Single Characters (by total number of strokes)

Characters in brackets [ ] are variant forms; characters in parentheses ( ) are simplified forms. The code after each character refers to the number of the radical and the number of strokes in the remainder. The numbers after the entries refer to lessons in WSC I.

1 stroke

一	1.0	yī, yí-, yì-	2

2 strokes

七	1.1	qī-, qí-	3
九	5.1	jiǔ	3
了	6.1	le	7
二	7.0	èr	2
人	9.0	rén	3
（儿）兒	10.0	ér, -r	7
八	12.0	bā, bá-	3
（儿）幾	16.0	jǐ-	2
十	24.0	shí	2
（厂）廠	27.0	chǎng	13

3 strokes

三	1.2	sān	2
（万）萬	1.2	-wàn	6
下	1.2	xià	9
上	1.2	shàng	9
（于）於	7.1	yú	13
（幺）麼	4.2	ma	3
久	4.2	jiǔ	12
也	5.2	yě	1
（习）習	5.2	xí	13
（飞）飛	5.2	fēi	9
（个）個	9.1	-gè, -ge	2
千	24.1	-qiān	6
大	37.0	dà	3
女	38.0	nǚ	4
子	39.0	zǐ	6
小	42.0	xiǎo	3
山	46.0	shān	2
工	48.0	gōng	12
（广）廣	53.0	guǎng	13

4 strokes

（开）開	1.3	kāi	10

不	1.3	bú-, bù- 1
(书)書	2.3	shū 1
中	2.3	zhōng 1
(为)爲	3.3	wèi 6
(长)長	4.3	cháng 8
五	7.2	wǔ 2
(从)從	9.2	cóng 9
(什)甚	9.2	shém- 3
今	9.2	jīn 10
六	12.2	liù 2
公	12.2	gōng 12
分	18.2	fēn 4
午	24.2	wǔ 10
(历)歷	27.2	lì 13
友	29.2	yǒu 4
太	37.1	tài 1
天	37.1	tiān 10
夫	37.1	fū, fu 12
少	42.1	shǎo 4
文	67.0	wén 3
方	70.0	fāng 9
日	72.0	rì 12
月	74.0	yuè 11
毛	82.0	máo 4
(气)氣	84.0	-qi 10

水	85.0	shuǐ 5
火	86.0	huǒ 9
父	88.0	fù 6
牛	93.0	niú 7
(車)	159.0	chē 7
5 strokes		
(东)東	1.4	dōng 8
(头)頭	3.4	tóu 7
(电)電	5.4	diàn 10
(们)們	9.3	-men 1
他	9.3	tā 1
以	9.3	yǐ 6
〔囬〕回	13.3	huí 2
(写)寫	14.3	xiě 6
出	17.3	chū 15
北	21.3	běi 8
半	24.3	bàn 12
去	28.3	qù 9
叫	30.2	jiào 5
可	30.2	kě 5
句	30.2	jù 13
史	30.2	shǐ 13
(叶)葉	30.2	yè 15
(台)臺	30.2	tái 14
四	31.2	sì 2

（礼）禮	113.1 lǐ 11	
（红）紅	120.3 hóng 15	
（约）約	120.3 yuē 10	
老	125.0 lǎo 8	
肉	130.0 ròu 7	
行	144.0 xíng 15	
西	146.0 xī 8	
（观）觀	147.2 guān 14	
（过）過	162.3 guò 11	
（问）問	169.3 wèn 5	

7 strokes

（来）來	1.6 lái 9
（两）兩	1.6 liǎng 2
些	7.5 xiē 4
你	9.5 nǐ 1
住	9.5 zhù 9
作	9.5 zuò 13
別	18.5 bié 11
助	19.5 zhù 15
告〔告〕	30.4 gào 7
吧	30.4 ba 9
〔呀〕啊	30.4 a 14
（听）聽	30.4 tīng 14
〔回〕回	31.4 huí 11

坐	32.4 zuò 9
（块）塊	32.4 kuài 4
姊	38.5 zǐ 6
（层）層	44.4 céng 14
希	50.4 xī 14
弟	57.4 dì 7
（张）張	57.4 zhāng 3
快	61.4 kuài 9
忘	61.3 wàng 13
我	62.3 wǒ 1
找	64.4 zhǎo 15
（报）報	64.4 bào 1
（时）時	72.3 shí 11
（条）條	75.3 -tiáo 7
每	80.3 měi 11
没〔沒〕	85.4 méi 2
汽	85.4 qì 7
〔牠〕它	93.3 tā 15
男	102.2 nán 4
究	116.2 jiū 14
（系）係	120.1 -xi 15
（纽）紐	120.4 niǔ- 10
（纸）紙	120.4 zhǐ 4
（诉）訴	149.5 -song, -su 7
走	156.0 zǒu 8

車（车）還	159.0 chē 7	
（还）還	162.4 hái 10	
（这）這	162.4 zhè 3,	
	zhèi 2,	
	zhèm- 6	
那〔那〕	163.4 ná 8, nǎ- 8,	
	nà- 3, něi- 2,	
	nèi- 2, nèm- 6	
里	166.0 lǐ 8	
（里）裏	166.0 lǐ, -li 8	
（饭）飯	184.4 fàn 5	

8 strokes

（画）畫	1.7 huà 4
事	6.7 shì 5
京	8.6 jīng 8
來（来）	9.6 lái, lai 9
兒（儿）	10.6 ér, r 7
兩（两）	11.6 liǎng 2
〔兩〕兩	11.6 liǎng 2
到	18.6 dào 9
（参）參	28.6 cān 14
呢	30.5 ne 7
和	30.5 hé 14
（图）圖	31.5 tú 15

（国）國	31.5 guó 1
（卖）賣	37.5 mài 4
姓	38.5 xìng 3
姐	38.5 jiě 6
妹	38.5 mèi 6
（学）學	39.5 xué 5
定	40.5 dìng 11
店	53.5 diàn 9
底	53.5 dǐ 14
念	61.4 niàn 8
房	63.4 fáng 8
所	63.4 suǒ 10
於（于）	70.4 yú 13
明	72.4 míng 10
朋	74.4 péng 4
東（东）	75.4 dōng 8
（极）極	75.4 jí 12
法	85.5 fǎ, fà 8
玩	96.4 wán 11
（现）現	96.4 xiàn 7
的	106.3 de 6
知	111.3 zhī 4
社	113.3 shè 13
（英）英	140.5 yīng- 3
（话）話	149.6 huà 3

長（长）   168.0 cháng 8
雨   173.0 yǔ 10
（鱼）魚   195.0 yú 7

9 strokes

（亲）親   3.8 -qin 6
信   9.7 xìn 12
係（系）   9.7 xì 15
前   18.7 qián 8
南   24.7 nán 15
〔城〕城   32.6 chéng 8
孩   39.6 hái 6
客   40.6 kè 12
封   41.6 fēng 12
屋   44.6 wū 10
很   60.6 hěn 1
後（后）   60.6 hòu 8
怎   61.5 zěn, zěm- 6
思   61.5 sī 7
拜   64.5 bài 11
是   72.5 shì 3
昨   72.5 zuó 11
星   72.5 xīng 14
〔爲〕爲   86.5 wèi 6
（点）點   86.5 diǎn 7

甚（什）   99.4 shén, shém 3
看   109.4 kàn 1
（研）研   112.6 yán 14
約   120.3 yuē 10
紅（红）   120.3 hóng 15
（给）給   120.6 gěi 4
美   123.3 měi 1
英（英）   140.5 yīng 3
（茶）茶   140.6 chá 5
要   146.3 yào 2
（觉）覺   147.5 jué 12
（说）説   149.7 shuō 3
（贵）貴   154.5 guì 1
香   186.0 xiāng 13
飛（飞）   183.0 fēi 9

10 strokes

們（们）   9.8 mén 1
個（个）   9.8 gè 2
候   9.8 hòu 11
哪〔哪〕   30.7 nǎ-, něi- 2
哥   30.7 gē 7
城   32.7 chéng 8
家   40.7 jiā 8
師（师）   50.7 shī 8

這（这）　162.7 zhè 3, zhèi- 2,
　　　　　　　　zhèm- 6

〔都〕都　163.8 dōu 2

（馆）舘　184.8 guǎn 8

魚（鱼）　195.0 yú 7

12 strokes

喜　30.9 xǐ 5

喝　30.9 hē 5

報（报）　32.9 bào 1

就　43.9 jiù 3

〔帮〕幫　50.9 bāng 15

幾（几）　52.9 jǐ 2

敢　66.8 gǎn 14

期　74.8 qī 14

湯（汤）　85.9 tāng 5

港　85.9 gǎng 13

（湾）灣　85.9 wān 14

爲（为）　87.8 wèi 6

畫（画）　102.7 huà 4

着（着）　109.7 zhe 15

筆（笔）　118.6 bǐ 4

給（给）　120.6 gěi 4

菜（菜）　140.8 cài 5

華（华）　140.8 huá 14

街　144.6 jiē 10

訴（诉）　149.5 sù, sòng 7

（谢）謝　149.10 xiè 15

貴（贵）　154.5 guì 1

買（买）　154.5 mǎi 1

（道）道　162.9 dào 4

都　163.9 dōu 2

（铺）舖　167.7 pù 8

開（开）　169.4 kāi 10

〔饭〕飯　184.4 fàn 5

黑　203.0 hēi 15

13 strokes

嗎（吗）　30.10 ma 1

塊（块）　32.10 kuài 4

想　61.9 xiǎng 4

愛（爱）　61.9 ài 6

意　61.9 yì 7

新　69.9 xīn 4

會（会）　73.9 huì 5, -huì 10

極（极）　75.9 jí 12

（楼）樓　75.9 lóu 9

筷　118.7 kuài 12

萬（万）　140.9 wàn 6

葉（叶）　140.9 yè 15

興（兴）   134.9 xīng, xǐng 11   20 strokes

舘（馆）   135.10 guǎn 8   覺（觉）   147.13 jué 12

親（亲）   147.9 qīn 6

豬（猪）   152.9 zhū 11   22 strokes

錢（钱）   167.8 qián 4   歡（欢）   76.18 huān 5

頭（头）   181.7 tóu 7   聽（听）   128.16 tīng 14

17 strokes   25 strokes

幫（帮）   50.14 bāng 15   灣（湾）   85.23 wān 14

聰（聪）   128.11 cōng 12   觀（观）   147.18 guān 14

謝（谢）   149.10 xiè 15

還（还）   162.13 hái 10

〔還〕還   162.13 hái 10

〔館〕舘   184.8 guǎn 8

點（点）   203.5 diǎn, diar 7

〔點〕點   203.5 diǎn 7

18 strokes

禮（礼）   113.3 lǐ 11

19 strokes

邊（边）   162.5 biān 15

關（关）   169.11 guān 13

難（难）   172.11 nán 6

願（愿）   181.10 yuàn 15

WRITTEN STANDARD CHINESE I

Vocabulary

(Numbers refer to lessons in <u>Written Standard Chinese, Vol. I</u>. Words not in-
uded in presupposed lessons are marked with an *. See Introduction.)

<u>A</u>

啊 P (question particle; exclamatory particle) 14

愛 AV love to, be fond of 6

<u>B</u>

八 NU eight 3

吧 P (sentence particle,
softens an imperative) 9

白 AT white 15

百 M hundred 6

白菜 N Chinese cabbage,
elery cabbage 15

白的 N something white;
hite 15

白天 TW daytime, during
he day 15

-bǎiwàn 百萬 M million 6

bàn 半 NU half 12

bāng 幫 V help, assist 15

bāng máng 幫忙 VO help, assist 15

bāngzhe 幫着 V help, assist 15

bāngzhu 幫助 V/N help, assist-
(ance) 15

bào 報 N newspaper 1

bàoshang 報上 PW on/in the newspaper 9

bàoshang shuō 報上説 IE
it says in the newspaper 9

běibian 北邊 PW north 15

Běijīng 北京 PW Peking 8

Běijīng Dàxué 北京大學 PW
Peking University 10

Běijīng Dōng Lù 北京東路 PW
Peking East Road 9

*Běijīng Lóu 北京樓 PW Peking House (restaurant) 9

Běijīng Xī Lù 北京西路 PW Peking West Road 9

Běipíng 北平 PW Peiping 15

-běn 本 M (bound volumes, books) 2

běnlái 本來 TW original time, originally 12

běnzi/r 本子／兒 N notebook 14

bǐ 筆 N writing implement 4

biān/r 邊（兒） N/M side 15; BF (suffix in placewords) 15

bié 別 AV (you) do not...! 11

biéde 別的 N other, remaining 12

bié kèqi (le). 別客氣（了）
IE Don't stand on ceremony.

biéren 別人 N other people, remaining people 12

bù. 不 . IE No. 14

bù-, bú- 不 A not 1

búdùi. 不對 . IE Wrong. 12

bùshǎo 不少 SV quite a few 8

búyào 不要 AV (you) do not...! 11

búyòng 不用 AV need not 12

bùzěmma 不怎麼 A not so, no all that 7

C

cài 菜 N vegetable; dish (of food)

cānguān 參觀 V visit (a place t examine its facilities) 14

-céng 層 M layer, story, level 14

chá 茶 N tea 5

cháng 長 SV long 8

Cháng Jiāng 長江 N Yangtze Riv 14

chē 車 N vehicle, car 7

chéng 城 N city 8

chénglǐtou/li 城裏頭（裏） PW the area inside the city; downtown

chéng wàitou 城外頭 PW the area outside the city 8

chī 吃 V eat, have...to eat 5

chī fàn 吃飯 VO have a meal, eat; eat rice 5

chu 出 VS so that the action emer from a place; out 15

chuán 船 N ship 9

chū lai 出來 V come out 15

chū qu 出去 V go out 15

cóng 從 CV from 9

cōngming 聰明 SV intelligent, bright 12

cóngqián 從前 TW the past; formerly 14

D

dà 大 SV big, great 3; old (in comparing ages of people) 7

dǎ diànhuà 打電話 VO make a telephone call 10

dàhòunian 大後年 TW three years from now 11

dàhòutian 大後天 TW three days from now 11

dào 到 V arrive 9; CV to 9; to 9; until 10; VS so that the actor arrives at the place-word object of the verb; so that the actor successfully achieves the action of the verb 13

dàqiánnian 大前年 TW three years ago 11

dàqiántian 大前天 TW three days ago 11

dǎsuan 打算 AV plan to 12

dàxué 大學 PW university 10

*dǎ zì 打字 VO write on a typewriter, type 10

*dǎzìjī 打字機 N typewriter 10

de 的 P (follows the modifier in a modifier-modified construction, where the modified element is a noun; also replaces this noun) 6

de 得／的 P (between a verb and a manner comment) 13

děi 得 AV must, have to, ought to 12

X de shihou(r) 的時候（兒） TW when X 11

dì- 第 SP (ordinalizing prefix) 10

*diànchē 電車 N trolley car 10

diànhuà 電話 N telephone 10

diànyǐng(r) 電影（兒） N movie, film 11

dìdi 弟弟 N younger brother 7

dìèr 第二   CA secondly 10

dìèrtiān 第二天   TW the second day, the next day 10

dìfang 地方   PW place; *space (available for use) 9

dìtú 地圖   N map 15

dǐxia 底下   PW area underneath 14

dìyī 第一   CA firstly 10

dōngběi 東北   PW northeast; Manchuria 15

dōngbian 東邊   PW east 15

*Dōngjīng 東京   PW Tokyo 8

Dōngjīng Dàxué 東京大學   PW Tokyo University 10

dōngnán 東南   PW southeast 15

dōng-nán-xī-běi 東南西北   IE north, south, east, west 15

dōngxi 東西   N thing, object 8

dōng-xī-nán-běi 東西南北   IE north, east, south, west 15

dōu 都   A in all cases 2

duì 對   SV correct, right 12

duì 對   CV (facing:) with respect to, to, in 13

duì le. 對了   . IE That's right. 12

duō 多   SV many, much 4, 7; M plus a fraction (of the preceding measure), and then some 4; A more 13

duō(ma), duó(ma) 多（麼）   A to what extent?, how? 4

duōshao 多少   N, NU how much?, how many? 4

E

èr 二   NU two 2

èryuè 二月   TW February 11

érzi 兒子   N son 7

F

Fàguo 法國   PW France 8

Fàguo huà 法國話   French (language) 8

fàn 飯   N cooked rice; food; meal 5

fàndiàn 飯店   N restaurant 9

-fānglǐ 方里   M square mile 9

fànguanzi/r 飯舘子／兒   N restaurant 8

fángzi 房子　　N building 8

Fǎwén 法文　　N French (language, literature) 8

fēi 飛　V fly 9; *fly to 13

fēichu lai/qu 飛出來／去　V fly out 15

fēidao 飛到　　V fly to 9

fēijī 飛機　　N airplane 9

-fēn 分　M cent 4

-fēng 封　M (letters) 12

fùmǔ 父母　N parents 6

fùqin 父親　N father 6

G

gǎn 敢　AV dare 14

gāo 高　SV high; tall 2

gàosu/song 告訴　V inform, tell 7

gāoxìng 高興　SV happy 11

-ge, -gè 個　M (single persons or objects) 2

gēge 哥哥　N older brother 7

gěi 給　V give 4; CV for, to 12

-gei 給　VS so that something is given to somebody, to 4

gēn 跟　CV with, accompanying; C and 10

gōngchǎng 工廠　N factory 13

gōngfu 工夫　N (free) time 12

gōnggòngqìchē 公共汽車　N (public) bus 12

gōnggòngqìchēzhàn 公共汽車站　N bus stop; bus station 12

gònghéguó 共和國　N republic 14

-gōnglǐ 公里　M kilometer 12

*gōngpíng 公平　SV fair, equitable 15

*gōngqián 工錢　N wage, pay 13

gōngren 工人　N laborer, worker 13

gōngshè 公社　N commune 13

gōngzuò 工作　N job 13; V to work 13

gòu 夠　SV/A sufficient(ly), enough 11

Guǎngzhōu 廣州　PW Canton 13

guānxi 關係　N connection, relevance 15

guānyu 關於　CV concerning, about 13

guì 貴 SV expensive 1

guì xìng? 貴姓   IE What is your

(honorable) surname? 3

guò 過 V pass, go by, after 12

-guò/guo 過 VS (completed action) 12

-guo 過 VS (at least one occurrence

of the action of the verb) 11

guójiā 國家   N nation, country 9

Guóxiān 國先   N Kuo-hsien (a

given name) 5

Guóxīn 國新   N Kuo-hsin (a given

name) 5

<u>H</u>

hái 還 A still, furthermore 10

hái méi(yǒu)...ne   還没（有）...

呢 A V... P have not ...yet,

still not... 10

háishi 還是   CA is (either)?,

or is? 12

háizi 孩子   N child 6

hǎo 好 SV good; well, healthy 1;

IE That will be fine. 1; A easy

to 10

hǎochī 好吃   SV tasty 5

*hǎohē 好喝 SV good to drink 5

hǎojǐ- 好幾   NU quite a few 8

hǎokàn 好看   SV good-looking;

*easy to read 2

hǎo shuō. 好説 . IE You flatter

me. 12

*hǎoxiē- 好些   NU quite a few 8

hǎozǒu 好走   SV easy to travel 8

hē 喝 V drink, have...to drink 5

hēdào 喝到   V drink as far as 13

hēide 黑的   N (something) black 1

hē jiǔ 喝酒   VO drink (alcohol) 7

hěn 很 A very 1; very much 5

hěn kuài 很快   MA very soon 9

hěn shǎo 很少   A (very) seldom 13

hépíng 和平   N peace 15

*hóngchá 紅茶   N black tea 15

hóngde 紅的   N (something) red 15

hóngyè 紅葉   N red leaves, colore

leaves (of autumn) 15

hòubian 後邊   PW back 15

hòunian 後年   TW year after next

11

hòutian 後天   TW day after

tomorrow 11

hòutou 後頭   PW back 8

huà 話 N speech, language 3

huà 畫 V draw, paint 7

huà(r) 畫（兒） N painting, picture 4

huà huà(r) 畫畫（兒） VO draw, paint 7

Huá Shān 華山 N Mt. Hua 14

huí 回 *V return to 13

huì 會 AV know how to, can 5

*huí jiā 回家 VO return home 11

huí lai/qu 回來／去 V come/go back 11

huí xìn 回信 VO send a letter in reply 13

huǒchē 火車 N train 9

huǒchēzhàn 火車站 PW railway station 9

J

jǐ 幾 NU *how many (under ten)?; a few, several (up to ten) 2

jì 寄 V mail 13

jiā 家 N family 8

jiā/jia 家 PW home 8

-jiā(r) 家（兒） M (shops, restaurants) 8

jiāli 家裏 PW home, family 8

jiāliren 家裏人 N people in the family 8

jiāng 江 BF Chiang 14

jiāo 教 V teach 6

jiào 叫 V be named 5; tell, ask (someone to do something) 12

jiāo shū 教書 VO teach 6

jìdào 寄到 V get to (by mail) 13

jiē 街 N street 10

jiějie 姐姐，姊姊 N older sister 6

jiěmèi 姐／姊妹 N (fellow) sister 6

jiēshang 街上 PW on the street; shopping district 10

jìgei 寄給 V mail to (someone) 13

jīhui 機會 N opportunity, chance 14

-jíle 極了 BF extremely 12

jīnnian 今年 TW this year 11

jīntian 今天 TW today 10

jiǔ 九 NU nine 3

jiǔ 酒 N wine, liquor, alcoholic beverage 5

jiǔ 久 SV long (time) 12

jiù 就 A only 3; then, afterwards 7; *exactly 8; right away 9; as a consequence, then 11

jiǔdiàn 酒店 N liquor store 9

jiǔpù 酒舖 N liquor store, wine shop 8

-jù 句 M (sentences) 13

juéde 覺得 V feel that, be of the opinion that 12

jùzi 句子 N sentence 13

kàndào 看到 V read to; see as far as 13

kè 課 N class 10; *M lesson 10

kèqi 客氣 SV polite, standing on ceremony 12

*kèren 客人 N guest 12

kěshi 可是 MA but 5

kéyi 可以 AV be permitted to, may, can, will 6

-kuài 塊 M dollar 4; piece 11

kuài 快 SV fast, quick 9; A quickly, soon 9; close to, nearly 13

kuàizi 筷子 N chopsticks 12

K

kāi 開 V drive; start away 10; open, begin operations 12; *CV driving, by 10

kāi chē 開車 VO drive (a car) 10

kāichu lai/qu 開出來／去 V drive out 15

kàn 看 V read 1; look at; think about, have the opinion that 7; visit, see (a person) 10

L

lái 來 V come 9; (come and) be here 11; come to 13

lai 來 P (sentence particle, indicates motion toward the speaker) 9

lǎo 老 SV venerable, elderly, old 1; BF (prefixed to surnames) 14

lǎopéngyou 老朋友 N old friend 14

lǎoshī　老師　N　teacher, tutor; Mr., Mrs., Miss (referring to a teacher) 8

-le 了　VS　(completed action) 10; P (sentence particle, indicates a change in state, or action completed in the past, having occurred as of the present) 7, 10

-lǐ 里　M　mile; Chinese mile 8

liǎng- 兩　NU　two 2

lǐbài 禮拜　TW　week 11

lǐbàièr 禮拜二　TW　Tuesday 11

lǐbàijǐ 禮拜幾　TW　what day of the week? 11

lǐbàitiān 禮拜天　TW　Sunday 11

lǐbàiyī 禮拜一　TW　Monday 11

lǐbian 裏邊　PW　inside 15

líng 零　NU　zero; and (in numbers) 14

lìshǐ 歷史　N　history 13

lǐtou 裏頭　PW　inside 8

liù 六　NU　six 2

lóu 樓　N　building of two or more stories 9; BF floor, story 9

lóu dǐxia 樓底下　PW　downstairs 14

lóushàng 樓上　PW　upstairs 9

lóuxià 樓下　PW　downstairs 9

lù 路　N　road; route, way 7

lǜde 綠的　N　something green; green 15

M

ma 嗎　P　(interrogative sentence particle) 1

-ma 麼　P　(interrogative suffix) 3

mǎi 買　V　buy, shop for 1

mài 賣　V　sell; be for sale; sell for 4

màigei 賣給　V　sell to 4

mǎimai 買賣　N　business, trade 5

màn 慢　SV/A　slow(ly) 9

máng 忙　SV/*V　busy; busy about; be in a rush 12

màn zǒu. 慢走　. IE Goodbye. 13

máo 毛　BF　Mao; *made of hair 4; M dime 4

*máobǐ 毛筆 N (Chinese) writing brush 4

méi- 没 A not (before yǒu) 2

měi- 每 SP each, every 11

Měiguo 美國 N America, the United States 1

mèimei 妹妹 N younger sister 6

méiqián 没錢 SV poor, impecunious 6

Měishēng 美生 N Mei-sheng (a given name) 5

méiyìsi 没意思 SV uninteresting, not fun 7

méiyou 没有 V there is not 4

méi(you) 没(有) A (negates completed action sentences) 10

méiyou guānxi. 没有關係 IE Never mind. 15

Měizhēn 美真 N Mei-chen (a given name) 5

-men 們 BF (indicates plural number) 1

míngbai 明白 V understand clearly 15

míngnian 明年 TW next year 11

míngtian 明天 TW tomorrow 10

míngzi 名子 N name, given name 5

mǔqin 母親 N mother 6

N

ná 拿 V grasp take in the hand; manipulate; take, bring 13; CV taking in the hand, with 13

nà 那 N that (topic only) 3

náli 哪／那裏, nǎr 哪／那兒 PW where? 8

nàli/nèr/-ner 那裏／那兒 PW there 8

nán 難 SV difficult, hard 6; A difficult to, hard to 6

nán- 男 AT male 4

nánbian 南邊 PW south 15

nánde 男的 N man 6

nánháizi 男孩子 N boy 6

Nánjīng 南京 PW Nanking 15

nánlǎoshī 男老師 N male teacher 8

nánpéngyou 男朋友 N male friend 4

nánxiánsheng 男先生 N male teacher 4

nánxuésheng　男學生　　　N　male

　　student 5

ne　呢　P　(at the end of a follow-up

　　question:) And...? 7; (continuative

　　sentence particle) 8

něi-　哪，那　SP　which? 2

nèi-　那　SP　that, those, the, the

　　other 2

nèige shíhou(r)　那個時候（兒）TW

　　that time (in the past) 11

nèi(yi)tiān　那（一）天　　TW

　　that day (in the past) 11

nèmma　那麼　　A　in that way; *to

　　that degree, so, such 6; CA　in

　　that case 13

néng　能　AV　be able to, can 5

nǐ　你　N　you (singular) 1

-nián　年　M　year 11

niàn　念　V　read, study 8

niàndào　念到　　V　read to / as

　　far as 13

*niánnián　年年　　A　every year 11

niàn shū　念書　　VO　read, study,

　　go to school 8

niú　牛　N　cow, ox, cattle 7

niúròu　牛肉　　N　*beef 7

Niǔyuē　紐約　　New York 10

nǚ-　女　AT　female 4

nǚde　女的　　N　woman 6

nǚér　女兒　　N　daughter 7

nǚháizi　女孩子　　N　girl 6

nǚlǎoshī　女老師　　N　female

　　teacher 8

nǚpéngyou　女朋友　　N　female

　　friend 4

nǚxiānsheng　女先生　　N　female

　　teacher 4

nǚxuésheng　女學生　　N　female

　　student 5

P

péngyou　朋友　N　friend 4

pùzi　舖子　N　shop, store 8

Q

qī　七　NU　seven 3

-qiān　千　M　thousand 6

qián　錢　N　money 4; BF　*Ch'ien 4

qián-　前　SP　past 13

qiánbian　前邊　　PW　front 15

qiánnian　前年　　TW　year before

last 11

qiántian　前天　　TW　day before

yesterday 11

qiántou　前頭　　PW　front 8

-qiānwàn　千萬　　M　ten million 6

qìchē　汽車　　N　automobile 7

qìchēzhàn　汽車站　　PW　bus

station 9

qǐng　請 V　request, invite 3

qìshuǐ, qìshuěr　汽水（兒）

N　carbonated soft drink, soda pop

12

qù　去　V　go, go to 13

qu　去　P　(sentence particle,

indicates motion away from the

speaker) 9

qùnian　去年　　TW　last year 11

R

rén　人　N　person 3

rénmín　人民　　N　the people (of

a country) 13

rénmíngōngshè　人民公社　　N

people's commune 13

-rì　日　*M　day (of the month)

(literary) 12

Rìběn　日本　　PW　Japan 12

ròu　肉　N　meat 7

S

sān　三　NU　three 2

shān　山　N　mountain, hill 2

shàng, -shang　上　L　top 9

-shang　上　VS　so that the action of

the verb proceeds upwards; up (with

lai and qu) 14

shàngbian　上邊　　PW　surface, top,

above 15

shàng chē　上車　　VO　get on a bus/

train/trolley, get into a car 12

shàng chuán　上船　　VO　get onto a

ship 12

shāngdiàn　商店　　store 14

shàng(ge)lǐbài　上（個）禮拜

TW　last week 11

shàng(ge)yuè　上（個）月　　TW　las

month 11

Shànghǎi 上海 PW Shanghai 13

shàng kè 上課 VO go to class 10

shàng lai 上來 V come up 12

shàng qu 上去 V go up 12

shàngtou 上頭 PW surface, top, above 9

shàngwu 上午 TW morning 10

shàng xué 上學 VO go to school 12

shàngyízhàn 上一站 PW the last stop (before now) 12

shǎo 少 SV few, little (in amount) 8; A less 13

shéi 誰 N who? whom? 3

shémma 甚麼 N what? 3

shēng 生 V be born 11

shēngrì 生日 N birthday 12

shí 十 NU ten 2

shì 是 V be 3; IE It is so. 5; *AV be true that 5

shì 事 N job 5

shíèryuè 十二月 TW December 11

shíhou(r) 時候（兒） TW time 11

shíjǐ 十幾 NU *ten plus how many?; ten plus a few 2

shìqing 事情 N job; matter, affair 12

shíwàn 十萬 NU a hundred thousand 6

shōu 收 V receive 13

shōudào 收到 V receive 13

shū 書 N book 1

shūdiàn 書店 N book store 9

shuí 誰 N who? whom? 3

shuǐ 水 N water 5

shuō 說 V speak; say 3; talk about 13

shuōdào 說到 V get to (in talking) 13

shuō huà 說話 VO *speak 3

shūpù 書舖 N bookstore 8

sì 四 NU four 2

sìbiān 四邊 PW all four sides, everywhere 15

-suǒ(r) 所（兒） M (buildings) 10

suóyi 所以 MA therefore 12

T

tā 他 N he, she 1

tā 她， N she 1

tā 它， N it 15

tài 太 A too, excessively 1

Táiběi 臺北 PW Taipei 14

tàitai 太太 N lady; wife; Mrs. 3

Táiwān/wan 臺灣 PW Taiwan 14

Táiwān Dàxué 臺灣大學

PW (National) Taiwan University 14

tāng 湯 N soup 5

-tiān 天 M day 10

tiānqi 天氣 N weather 10

-tiáo 條 M (long things; roads; fishes) 7

tīng shuō 聽説 V (I) hear (it said) that 14

tīngzhe. 聽着 IE Listen. 15

tóngchē 同車 N being in the same vehicle 11

tóngchuán 同船 N being on the same ship 11

tóng(fēi)jī 同（飛）機 N being in the same airplane 11

tóngmíng 同名 N having the same given name 11

tóngshì 同事 N colleague 11

tóngwū 同屋 N roommate 11

tóngxìng 同姓 N having the same surname 11

tóngxué 同學 N fellow student; (term of address for someone in the same school as the speaker) 11

-tóu 頭 M (certain domestic animals, vegetables) 7; SP the first 13

-tou 頭 P (suffixed to a localizer, forms a place word) 8

túshūguǎn 圖書舘 N library 16

W

wàibian 外邊 PW outside 15

wàiguo 外國 N foreign (country), non-Chinese (country) 8

wàitou 外頭 PW outside 8

wán/r 玩（兒） V play, have fun, have a good time, play with 11

wǎn 晚 *SV late 11

-wàn 萬 M ten thousand 6

wǎnfàn 晚飯 N supper 10

wàng le 忘了 V forget 13

*Wànlǐchángchéng　萬里長城

  PW　(ten-thousand li long wall:)

  the Great Wall 13

wǎnshang　晚上　TW　evening 10

-wànwàn　萬萬　M　hundred

  million 6

wèishemma　爲甚麼　MA　for

  what reason?　why? 6

wèn　問　V　ask 5

wènwen　問問　V　make a few in-

  quiries 5

wǒ　我　N　I 1

wǒ bùgǎn shuō.　我不敢説　IE

  I don't know. 14

wǔ　五　NU　five 2

*wǔfàn　午飯　N　noon meal, lunch

  10

wūzi　屋子　N　room 10

X

xià　下　L　bottom 9

-xia　下　VS　so that the action of

  the verb proceeds downwards; down

  (with lai and qu) 14

xiàbian　下邊　PW　bottom, below 15

xià chē　下車　VO　get off a bus/

  train/trolley, get out of a car 12

xià chuán　下船　VO　get onto a ship

  12

xià(ge)lǐbài　下（個）禮拜　TW

  next week 11

xià(ge)yuè　下（個）月　TW　next

  month 11

xià kè　下課　VO　get out of class 10

xià lai　下來　V　come down 12

xiān　先　A　first, beforehand, earlier 3

xiǎng　想　V　think; *think of 4; AV

  have it in mind to, intend to 4

xiǎngdào　想到　V　think, imagine 13

Xiānggǎng　香港　PW　Hong Kong 13

xiānsheng　先生　N　gentleman;

  husband; Mr. 3

xiànzài　現在　TW　the present, now 7

xiǎo　小　SV　small 3

Xiǎofāng　小方　N　Hsiao-fang (a

  given name) 15

xiǎoháizi　小孩子　N　child 6

xiǎohár　小孩兒　N child 7

*Xiǎo Hóngshū　小紅書　N　Little Red

  Book (of quotations from Mao Tse-tung)

  15

xiǎojie   小姐   N young lady, Miss 6

Xiǎopíng   小平   N Hsiao-p'ing (a given name) 15

xiǎoshuō(r)   小説（兒）   N fiction; work of fiction; novel 13

xià qu   下去   V go down 12

xiàtou   下頭   PW bottom, below 9

xiàwu   下午   TW afternoon 10

xià xué   下學   VO get out of school 12

xiàyízhàn   下一站   PW the next stop 12

xià yǔ   下雨   VO to rain 10

xīběi   西北   PW northwest 15

xībian   西邊   PW west 15

-xiē   些   M, NU a few, a small amount of some 4

xiě   寫   V write 6

xiědào   寫到   V write as far as 13

*xiégei   寫給   V write to 12

xièxie.   謝謝   . IE Thanks. 15

xiě xìn   寫信   VO write (letters) 12

*xiězai   寫在   V write at 9

xiě zì   寫字   VO write 6

xǐhuan   喜歡   V like 5; AV like to 5

xīn 新   SV new 4; A newly, recently

xìn 信   N letter 12

xīnán   西南   PW southwest 15

*xìnfēng(r)   信封（兒）   N envelope 12

xíng. 行   . IE It is acceptable / OK. 15

xìng 姓   N surname 3; V be surnamed

Xīngǎng   新港   PW New Haven 13

xīngqī   星期   N week 14

xīngqīèr   星期二   TW Tuesday 1

xīngqīrì/-tiān   星期日／天   TW Sunday 14

xīngqīyī   星期一   TW Monday 14

xìngqu   興趣   N interest 13

xīwàng   希望   V/N hope, wish 14

xué 學   V study, learn 6; AV study how to, learn how to 6

xuédào   學到   V study as far as 1

xuésheng   學生   N student 5

xuéwen   學問   N learning, knowled 14

*xuéxi 學習 V study 13

xuéxiào 學校 N school 6

Y

ya 呀 P (question particle, exclamatory particle) 14

yánjiu 研究 V study, do research on; N study, research 14

yánjiu xuéwen 研究學問 VO do research 14

yào 要 V want 2; require (as payment) 4; order (a dish in a restaurant) 5; AV want to 2; be about to, be going to 9

yàoshi 要是 MA if 11

yě 也 A also, too, either 1

yèzi 葉子 N leaf (of a tree, etc.) 15

yī 一 NU one, a, an 2; as soon as, once 7

yibàn/r 一半（兒） N half 12

*yìbiān X, yìbiān Y 一邊 X, 一邊 Y IE X and Y at the same time 15

yìdiǎn/r 一點（兒） NU-M a little, a bit of; some 7

yídìng 一定 A definitely, certainly 11

yídìng yào 一定要 A AV must, have to 11

yígòng 一共 A altogether, in all 12

yǐhòu 以後 TW afterward, after, from now on 12

yìhuǐ(r) 一會（兒） TW a **little** while, a moment 10

yíkuàr 一塊兒 PW one place 10; A together 10

Yīngguo 英國 N England 3

-Yīnglǐ 英里 M English mile 8

Yīngwén 英文 N English (language) 3

yīnwei 因爲 CA because 11

yǐqián 以前 TW previously, before 12

yìsi 意思 N meaning 7

yòng V 用 use 12; CV using, with 12

yǒu 有 V have 2; there is 4

yǒu bāngzhu 有幫助 SV helpful 15

yǒude　有的　N some 6

yǒude rén　有的人　N some people 6

yǒu(de) shíhou(r)　有（的）時候（兒）　sometimes 11

yǒumíng　有名　SV famous, well-known 6

yǒuqián　有錢　SV rich, wealthy 6

yǒuren　有人　N some people 6

yǒu xìngqu　有興趣　SV interesting 13; AV be interested in 13

yǒu xīwàng　有希望　SV promising 14

yǒu xuéwen　有學問　SV learned 14

yǒu yánjiu　有研究　SV well versed 14

yǒu yìdiǎn/r /yǒu diǎn/r 有一點（兒）有一點（兒）　A a bit 13

yǒuyìsi　有意思　SV interesting, fun 7

yǒu yìtiān　有一天　CA one day 11

*yú　魚　N fish 7

yǔ　雨　N rain 10

yuànyi　願意　AV want to 15

yuè　月　N month 11; M (in names of months) 11

Z

zài　再　A again, then (in the future) 11

zài　在　CV at 7; V be located at 8; A be...ing 8

-zai　在　VS so that the actor or the recipient of the action of the verb i located at; at 9

zài jiā　在家　VO be at home 8

zài yíkuàr　在一塊兒　CV O together 10

zǎo　早　SV early 10

zǎofàn　早飯　N breakfast 10

zǎoshang　早上　TW morning 10

zěmma　怎麼　A in what way? how? 6 MA how come? 10

zhàn　站　N/M station (for trains, etc.) 9

-zhāng　張　M (pieces of paper, table 4; BF Chang 3

zhǎo 找   V   look for; call on, visit 15

zhè 這   N   this (topic only) 3

-zhe 着   VS   (used in affirmative commands; indicates continuing action) 15

zhèi- 這   SP   this, these, the 2

zhèli, zhèr, -zher 這裏，這兒   PW   here 8

zhèmma 這麼   A   in this way; *to this degree, so, such 6

zhēn 真，   A   truly 1

zhèng 正   A   just (now) exactly, be right in the process of ...-ing 15

zhèng hǎo. 正好   IE   Just right. 15

zhèngshi/zai 正是／在   A   just (during), exactly (during) 15

Zhenzhēn 真真   N   Chen-chen (a given name) 5

zhǐ 紙   N   paper 4

zhīdao 知道   V   know 4

zhǐdiàn 紙店   N   stationery store 9

zhǐpù 紙舖   N   stationery store 8

zhōngfàn 中飯   N   lunch 10

Zhōngguo 中國   N   China 1

*Zhongguochéng 中國城   N   China-town 8

Zhōngguo huà 中國話   N   Chinese (language) 3

Zhōnghuá Mínguó 中華民國   N   Republic of China 14

Zhōnghuá Rénmín Gònghéguó 中華人民共和國   N   People's Republic of China 14

Zhōng-Měi Shūdiàn 中美書店   N   China-America Bookstore 9

*Zhōngshān 中山   BF   Chung-shan (sobriquet of Sun Yat-sen) 9

Zhōngshān Běi Lù 中山北路   PW   Chung-shan North Road 9

Zhōngwén 中文   N   Chinese (language) 3

zhōngwu 中午   TW   noon 10

Zhōngxīng Lóu 中興樓   PW   Revival House (restaurant) 11

zhū 豬   N   pig 11

zhù 住   V   reside, live; live at 9

zhūròu   N   豬肉   pork 11

zhuzai 住在   V   live at 9

zì 字 N (written) character,

  letter, word 6

*zǐmèi   姊妹   N (fellow) sister

  6

zǒu 走 V take (a route/road) 8;

  depart 10; be away 11; walk, go 14;

  VS so that the recipient of the

  action of the verb moves away from

  the speaker; away 14

zǒuchu lai/qu   走出來／去

  V walk out 15

zǒudao   走到   V walk to, go to

  14

zuò 做 V do; prepare (food) 5

zuò 坐 V sit; use as a means of

  conveyance 9; CV by (a means of

  conveyance) 9

zuò cài   做菜   VO prepare a

  dish (of food) 5

zuò fàn   做飯   VO cook 5

zuò mǎimai   做買賣   VO be in

  business 5

zuò shì   做事   VO work 5

zuótian   昨天   TW yesterday 11

zuòzai   坐在   V sit at 9